ZITS & *Glitz* & BODY BITS

JEANNE WILLIS & LYDIA MONKS

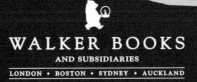

WALKER BOOKS
AND SUBSIDIARIES
LONDON • BOSTON • SYDNEY • AUCKLAND

CONTENTS

Part five · Zits

Spots, slap and hair stuff – sorted!

Part Six

Glitz

How not to look pants in clothes.

Part Seven

Soulmates

Friendly advice on being best buds, and how to keep it that way.

Part Eight

Sex & Snogs

A guide to boy's minds, hearts and dangly bits.

Bits
Boobs
& Blobs

Part One

Bits

"Am I just
a teenage
dirt bag?"

All the nitty-gritty on
growing up and private parts

6

Q Eek! My body is changing – am I morphing into an alien?

It seems unlikely, but just to make sure, check your symptoms against this chart.

AM I MORPHING INTO AN ALIEN?

1A Have you grown six heads? ☐

1B Is your face getting longer and less babyish? ☐

2A Is your skin green and oozing slime? ☐

2B Is your skin slightly shiny/spotty? ☐

3A Are you covered in thick, green fur? ☐

3B Are you growing little hairs under your arms/down your pants? ☐

4A Are you 50 light-years old? ☐

4B Are you between 8 and 17 years old? ☐

5A Have you recently destroyed another galaxy in a fit of rage? ☐

5B Do you sometimes feel a bit moody and misunderstood? ☐

6A Have you grown a tentacle overnight? ☐

6B Are you growing bumps on your chest? ☐

If you ticked mostly As – You are turning into an alien. Go back to your planet and take your spaceship with you!

If you ticked mostly Bs – YAY! You're turning into a woman. Welcome to the wonderful world of puberty!

Q Ooer! I couldn't tick any As or Bs – what's puberty? Puberty is when your body stops being like a child's and you start to become an adult. The time when it happens is called adolescence. Don't worry if you haven't noticed any changes yet – lots of girls reach puberty when they're about 11, but it can happen any time between 8 and 17.

Q Help! How can I tell if I've started puberty?

Some of the changes take place inside you, but others are more obvious. Don't panic – you won't grow a pair of big blancmanges overnight. The changes happen over several years so you've got ages to get used to the gorgeous new grown-up you. Here are some signs to look out for:

1 YOU START GROWING REALLY FAST. Up to 11 cm in one year! Yep, great excuse for buying new clothes!

2 YOUR HIPS GROW WIDER. To make room for a baby one day/to make your bum look cute.

3 YOUR VOICE GETS DEEPER. So you can shout at your parents/whisper sweet nothings in someone's ear.

4 YOUR FACE CHANGES SHAPE. So you look old enough to see an 18 film/have more room to put make-up on!

5 YOUR MUSCLES GET STRONGER. So you can carry your shopping.

6 YOUR BREASTS START TO DEVELOP. To feed babies/fill your bikini.

7 YOU GROW HAIR IN FUNNY PLACES. God's little joke – no good reason except to increase sales of razors/wax.

8 YOUR PERIODS START. So you can make babies/have an excuse to be moody once a month.

9 YOUR FEELINGS AND EMOTIONS CHANGE. So you can fall in love/fight for your rights/feel like a woman.

growth!

deep voice

wide hips

face shape

breasts

hair

periods

Q Help! I'm the shortest girl in my class. I'm sick of being called Titch, and the last time I went to the cinema they wouldn't let me in because I didn't look old enough.

HEY, Shorty!

It can be tough being short – it sometimes feels like everyone's looking down on you. People often assume short people are younger than they are – great when you're 40 but a pain in the butt when you're trying to get into a film that's not a cartoon about fairies.

But listen, it can be just as tough being tall. Everyone expects you to act older than you really are, and trousers are always too short in the leg. At least you can snip the bottoms off yours. Also, don't forget, you haven't finished growing yet if you're under 18. In the meantime, remember there are lots of good things about being a little person. Oh, and next time you go to the flicks, carry some ID to prove you're a big girl really.

GET THIS!
The average British woman is 1.62 m (5 foot 4 inches) tall.

10 GOOD THINGS ABOUT BEING TALL

1 You can reach the top shelf without a ladder.

2 You can get into X-rated movies. (Not that you'd ever do such a thing.)

3 You look great in long skirts.

4 You can look down on people.

5 Everyone wants you in the netball team.

6 Most of the boys in your class have to look up to you.

7 You can borrow your mum's clothes. (She must have some cool ones somewhere.)

8 You are brilliant at the high jump.

9 People think twice about picking on you.

10 You don't have to wear high heels.

GET THIS!

The tallest woman in history was Zeng Jinlian (born 1964, in central China). She was 2.48 m (just over 8 foot).

10 GOOD THINGS ABOUT BEING SMALL

1 You have less far to fall.

2 You can get away with a kid's fare on the bus. (Not that you'd ever do such a thing.)

3 Small trainers are cheaper than big ones in the same style.

4 You're never too tall for the guy you fancy.

5 Short people often make great leaders.

6 Your hair doesn't get caught in the springs if you sleep in the bottom bunk.

7 You save pounds on material if you make your own gear.

8 Boys like rescuing you.

9 There's always room for a little one.

10 You have a fantastic excuse for wearing high heels.

The shortest was Pauline Musters ("Princess Pauline", born 1876, in Holland). She was only 61 cm (24 inches) high.

Q Every time I throw a moody, my mum says it's my hormones – what's she cackling on about?

Hormones are chemicals in your body that tell it to behave in a certain way. At puberty, sex hormones kick-start all the physical changes that happen to you. They can also affect your emotions. Sometimes they take a while to settle down and you get mood swings. One minute, you're a ray of sunshine, the next, you want to strangle your own mother. Some mothers deserve to be strangled, of course, but mostly they don't mean to wind you up. When your hormones are mucking about, everybody seems out to get you – even the hamster.

Next time you feel like you're going to explode/cry/kill, remember that the food at The Correction Home for Moody Cows really sucks, put that axe down, and try these mood-calming tricks instead:

MOOD-CALMING TRICKS FOR MAD MOMENTS

* Beat the fluff out of your pillow.
* Dance like a lunatic/go for a run/walk the dog.

* Phone a friend and ask her to talk you down off the ceiling.
* Have a good howl.
* Pamper yourself.
* Put all your feelings down on paper, then tear it into tiny shreds.
* Count to 10.
* Cuddle someone you love.

Q I got a detention for calling someone a twat at school – why? I thought it just meant the same as twit.

Oops – what a difference one letter makes! Twat is a slang word for ladies' rude bits, and it's not a very pretty one either. There are loads of them. Some are quite sweet. Others are very rude. Some are simply disgusting! For your eyes only, here is a list...

> WARNING!!! Some people find these words very offensive, so don't use them in polite company.

Q Um, er, so what's the PROPER name for my front bottom?

Most of us have pet names for our privates (see below), but there comes a time when a girl needs to know what's what. Basically, external sex organs (the ones you can see) are called genitals. The proper name for female genitals is the vulva. The best way to see what yours looks like is to examine it gently with clean fingers using a hand mirror.

(Don't try this in Topshop! Find a place with good lighting where you know you won't be disturbed.)

fanny   honeypot   jelly roll
beaver   poontang   hole
box   vadge   muff
pussy
tail   slit   mivvy
quim
twat   cunt   bush
minge
snatch   flap
pad   shrubbery   coochie
crack

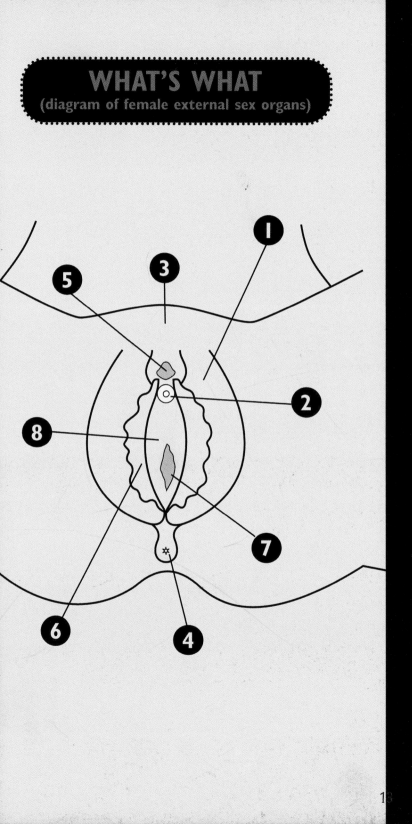

WHAT'S WHAT
(diagram of female external sex organs)

1. OUTER LABIA: Two thick folds of skin with pubic hair growing on them – these protect the inside of your vulva.

2. URINARY OPENING: The opening to the tube leading from your bladder (urethra).

3. MONS: A pad of fat that protects your pubic bone.

4. ANUS: Hole at the end of the digestive tract, where solid waste (poo) comes out.

5. CLITORIS: Very sensitive to touch. It becomes erect – the female equivalent of a penis.

6. INNER LABIA: Thin, hairless inner lips. They are rarely the same size and sometimes stick out. They make lubricating fluid in their glands, which is why they feel moist.

7. VAGINAL OPENING: Tube leading to your internal reproductive organs. It's where the blood comes out when you have a period, where a man puts his penis when you have sex, and where babies come out when they are born. (It may look small but it's very streeeeeeetchy!)

8. HYMEN: Thin layer of skin that partially covers the vaginal opening. An unbroken hymen used to be seen as a sign of virginity, but it isn't – hymens often break during puberty, especially if you play lots of sport.

Q *This is a bit of a hairy one: my sister has curly pubes but mine are dead straight and wispy – how weird is that?*

Not at all, actually. Pubic hair usually starts off soft and downy. As you get older, it often grows coarse and curly, but there is a fantastic variety of "Downstairs Hairdos". Sometimes it grows a completely different shade from the hair on your head. (This is Mother Nature's way of stopping folk checking your pubes to see if you're a natural blonde.)

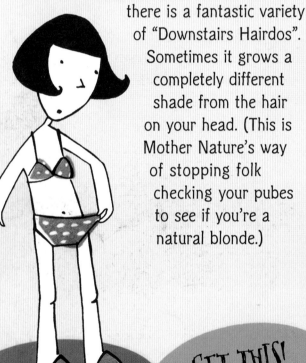

GET THIS!
The average vagina is 10 cm (4 inches) long.

A Girl's Guide to Downstairs Hairdos

1. THE SMOOTHY: pre-pubescent

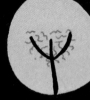

2. THE MUFTY TUFTY: scanty blond pubic hair; new growth

3. THE BUBBLE CUT: medium blond curls

4. THE BURNING BUSH: long, fine bushy red hair

5. THE MEXICAN WAVE: thick, black curls

6. THE CURLY-WURLY: profuse, sprawling brown hair

7. SHORT BACK AND SIDES: short, brown, neat triangle

8. THE MOHICAN: grows in neat strip down middle

14

Q Help! I smell funny down there – is there something wrong with me?

Depends what you mean by funny. A vagina smells kind of musky and salty, even if it's just been washed. Sometimes your natural odour is stronger on certain days, depending on the time of the month. It's caused by sweat, oil glands and cheeky little substances called pheromones, which are carried in your vaginal fluid and are highly attractive to the opposite sex. If you notice a nasty smell (often with an unusual discharge) you may have an infection. If you think you might have, see a doctor. She'll have seen it all before and will be able to treat it easily.

GET THIS! The French use less soap than any other country in Europe.

Q How am I supposed to wash right up inside my vagina?

You aren't! Vaginas are like posh ovens – they clean themselves! They produce special lubricating fluid that does the job perfectly. There's no need to go poking about. All you need to do is bath or shower daily, washing gently between your legs with mild soap – don't use fancy smellies on your delicate bits as it can cause irritation.

If you need to freshen up and you can't get to a shower, give yourself a quick going-over with a soapy flannel or paper towel (rinse carefully and pat dry) or keep some baby wipes in your bag. You can buy special wipes for your feminine area but it's best to avoid the ones with deodorant and perfume.

HOW TO CARE FOR YOUR MUFF

- ☐ HAND WASH ONLY
- ☐ DO NOT USE STRONG DETERGENT
- ☐ DO NOT DRIP-DRY
- ☐ DO NOT RUB HARD
- ☐ PAT DRY WITH CLEAN TOWEL
- ☐ DO NOT DRY-CLEAN
- ☐ DO NOT IRON
- ☐ DO NOT KEEP IN NASTY NYLON KNICKS
- ☐ KEEP IN COTTON UNDIES AND CHANGE DAILY

Q Help! I've got armpits like King Kong. Should I shave?

Some people find armpit hair very attractive, but if you don't like it, that's your business. Get rid! There are several ways of removing hair from your face and body, but before you reach for the razor/lawnmower/hedge-clippers, check out the advantages and disadvantages of each method.

GET THIS!
Humans are related to apes and used to have hair all over their bodies.

What	How	Pros	Cons
DRY SHAVING Best for armpits, legs.	Buy an electric razor for women. Plug in, switch on and shave your woolly bits.	Quick, easy and you can't cut yourself.	Some girls reckon electric razors don't leave skin as smooth.
WET SHAVING Best for armpits, legs.	Get an easy-grip razor or use a disposable one. Lather skin with mild soap and warm water. Shave downwards for pits, upwards for legs.	Quick, cheap, painless and easy to do yourself.	Hair grows back prickly within a few days. It's easy to nick yourself.
SALON WAXING Best for everywhere.	Make an appointment, take your trousers off and lie on the bed in old pants.	Hair doesn't grow back for six weeks. A beautician can reach those awkward places. No mess to clear up.	Pricey. Also, hairs have to be long enough for the wax to grip them.
HOME COLD WAXING Best for everywhere.	Use strips of ready-waxed Cellophane that you press onto your skin and pull off.	Cheaper than hot wax, quite effective and you can't burn yourself.	Can be painful and messy. Doesn't work on coarse hair.
HOME HOT WAXING Best for everywhere.	Wax is usually heated in a microwave or a pan of hot water. You spread warm wax onto your skin, press cotton strips onto the wax and whisk the hairs off.	Good results if done properly. Hair doesn't grow back for four to six weeks and it grows back soft.	Can be messy, painful and awkward. Risk of scalding with hot wax.
TWEEZING Best for eyebrows, odd stray hairs.	Buy good quality tweezers. Gently stretch skin, grab hair between tweezers and pull quickly in direction of growth.	Quick, cheap and effective.	Can be slightly painful and the hair will grow back within days.
HAIR-REMOVING CREAM Best for pits, legs, bikini	Always do a patch test first. Smooth cream onto hair	Cheap, painless and can give good results. Effects last	Messy and poo-eeh! Who cut the egg sandwiches?

Q Why does my body have to change? I don't want to grow up!

The reason your body changes is so that one day you can have babies. OK, maybe you'd rather poke pins in your eyes than think about that right now, but hang on a mo – the other thing about growing up is that your mind changes too. And guess what? You'll find yourself wanting to do all the squelchy stuff that used to make you go Yeeeuch! (Honestly, you will!)

True, growing up isn't always a breeze. Most girls (and boys) feel confused and upset at times, but it can also be the best fun you've ever had – if Peter Pan knew what he was missing he'd grow up like a shot!

Remember, you don't have to stop being you just because your body is changing. You can still do everything you love and more!

GET THIS!
The longest beard grown by a lady belonged to Janice Deveree (born 1862). It was 36 cm (14 inches) long.

GOOD THINGS ABOUT GROWING UP

- ✪ You can climb trees, jump in puddles and wear high heels. (Not all at the same time though!)

- ✪ You hold Mum's hand because you love her – not because you're crossing a road.

- ✪ You're never too old for a goodnight cuddle, but you can stay up late.

- ✪ You fall in love with a real person instead of a poster.

- ✪ You get to travel a whole lot further than the postbox.

- ✪ You get to make your own decisions – even if they suck.

- ✪ You can be who you want – it's your life!

Part Two

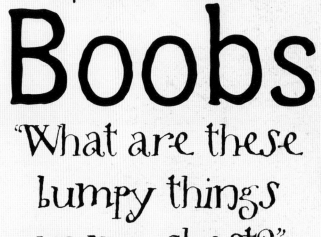

Boobs

"What are these lumpy things on my chest?"

How to be bosom buddies with your breasts

Q My brother says my boobs are just made of fat? Is that true?

No, that's what his head is made of. There's a lot more to breasts than meets the eye – show him the diagram below if he doesn't believe you.

MAMMARIES ARE MADE OF THIS

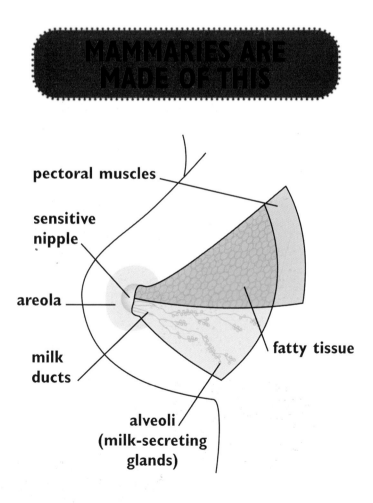

pectoral muscles

sensitive nipple

areola

milk ducts

fatty tissue

alveoli (milk-secreting glands)

ILLUSTRATION OF BREAST DEVELOPMENT

a) First, the nipple and the areola get larger and sometimes darker. (They might ache a bit.)

b) Milk ducts and fat tissue form a small, disc-like mound under each nipple and areola. This makes them stick out. (Don't be surprised if one forms before the other – it often happens.)

c) Fat deposits begin to fill out the area and your breasts may start to look pointy. (Maybe a good time to check out the bra counter.)

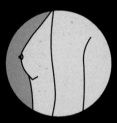

d) Breasts continue to fill out. Sometimes the nipples and areolas form a separate mound and get more pronounced. (Not always, though.)

e) You've got the full set!

Q Help! I'm flat-chested, but my nipples are tender and swollen. Why?

Don't worry! This often happens when your breasts start to develop. Your nipples grow first and they can feel a bit sore at the beginning, but it'll soon pass, promise! In the meantime, try not to knock them when you play netball and fold your arms in the dinner queue to protect them. If they're really killing you, ask your mum for some paracetamol.

Q Mum said she used to have really big boobs till she had me - is she making it up?

What? You don't believe your own mother?! Of course, she could be boasting, in which case the only way to tell for sure is to find a photo of her in a bikini in the olden days. Be warned though, she's probably telling the truth. Bosoms have a habit of changing shape and size during adulthood. Going on the pill, having a baby, or pigging out on cakes can all affect breast size and shape. Sometimes they get smaller; sometimes they get bigger. Some girls even go up a whole cup size just before their period.

Q Help! One of my boobs is bigger than the other. Am I a freak?

No, no, you are not turning into the Hunchfront of Notre Dame. One breast often grows faster than the other, but the other one soon catches up. Having said that, nobody - but nobody - has a truly matching pair, except Barbie (unless they're cheating).

I feel a right tit!

There once was a girl from Devizes
Whose **BOOBIES** were different sizes.
The one on the right
She would keep out of sight,
But the other won several prizes.

Q I'm a tomboy. Bosoms don't suit me. What use are they?

You're not the first to ask this question. Amazon women used to cut off their right boobs just so they could fire their arrows straight. True, breasts can get in the way when you're trying to fire an arrow – the upside is that bras make great catapults.

Seriously, Mother Nature didn't give you two bumps on the front for nothing – their main purpose is to make milk. Without it, humans would have died out long ago. OK, you can buy formula milk today, but breastfeeding is thought to be much better for the baby. Breasts also heighten your sexual pleasure, and boys think they're beautiful – even really intelligent boys – and anything that helps you catch your ideal mate has to be good.

Q Help! In winter my nipples stick out and show through my clothes.

Nipples are even better than seaweed at predicting a cold snap, hence the phrase "It's a bit nippy!" They are one of the most sensitive parts of a woman's body.

If it's cold or they are touched, tiny muscles make them go hard (erect). There's nothing you can do to stop it happening. But if you feel embarrassed, avoid tight-fitting tops, cover up with a jacket or wear a T-shirt/vest under your blouse. If it happens during swimming lessons, covering up with a cardy is a no-no. Just take a deep breath and jump in quick! Chances are, no one will notice, and anyway, everyone else's will be sticking out like hat pegs too!

Q My friend says our breasts will fill up with milk when we reach puberty – is it true?

No! You can't make any milk unless you have a baby. The milk-making glands (alveoli) in your breasts don't start working until you become pregnant.

Q I'm 14 and my breasts are really titchy. Will they grow any bigger?

Probably. Breasts don't usually reach their full size until you're about 17. Having said that, some of us are never going to be well endowed. If you want your breasts to look bigger, there's no need to stuff a pair of socks down your vest. The right bra can work wonders!

GET THIS!

Boys' breasts sometimes swell slightly at puberty – but this soon disappears when their hormones settle down. AH, BLESS!

OOOH John, what a lovely pair!

BRA STYLES

Underwired bra

Bra with gel inserts

Push-up bra

Bra with adjustable cleavage

In 1943, actress Jane Russell wore a famous uplift metallic bra in The Outlaw. The film was kept off screen for 6 years for reasons of morality!

Large breasts can weigh over a **pound**!

Q Help! My boobs are massive. I can't see my feet!

Some girls dream of having big breasts (boys dream about them constantly), but it's no fun if you feel uncomfortable with your body. Even so, don't try and hide your breasts by hunching your shoulders and staring at the floor. It will just give you lousy posture and you'll bash into lampposts.

The best thing to do is buy a bra with really good support. If you can't find what you want in the shops, try catalogues or the Internet. There are lots of gorgeous bras especially made for bigger-busted girls who don't want to look like their granny – you can even buy styles that "minimize" your bust. Once you've found your perfect bra, put your shoulders back, look the world in the eye and be confident!

There was a young lady called Marge
Whose boobs were as BIG as a barge.
Her twin sister, Jeannie,
Had bosoms so weeny
The boys called them Little and LARGE!

GET THIS!
The term brassière first appeared in American Vogue in 1907.

24

Q I'm 15, I'm flat-chested and I'm fed up

Remember that you haven't finished growing yet. The way you feel about your body is bound to change as you grow older. Having small breasts may feel like the end of the world right now, but true happiness doesn't lie in a whopping great pair of bosoms. Ask anyone who's got them. It may make boys notice you more, but wouldn't you rather they noticed your massive personality? If you still feel worried about it in a few years' time, discuss it with your doctor.

You could try wearing breast-enhancers. These are gel-filled moulds that you wear inside your bra to boost you up a few cup sizes. They look a bit like chicken fillets, but under clothes they look and feel like the real thing.

Q I'm sure my boobs are a funny shape. What should they look like?

There are no rules! Breasts come in all different shapes and sizes – just as well, 'cos some folk fancy fried eggs while others go wild for watermelons. Breasts vary more

in appearance than any other part of a woman's body. Even nipples come in a variety of fashionable shades from Barely Black to Princess Pink.

Q Help! I swear I'm a 34B but my bra keeps riding up at the back while my boobs are squishing out of the cups.

According to recent surveys, one in three women wears the wrong-sized bra. To avoid making the same boob, you need to measure yourself properly. See page 26 to find out how.

HOW TO FIND YOUR BRA SIZE

When you buy a bra, you need to know your chest measurement and cup size.

TO FIND YOUR CHEST SIZE

Measure just under your breasts around your rib cage and add 12 cm (5 inches).

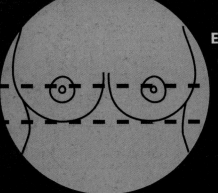

Example: 68 cm (27 inches) + 12 cm (5 inches) = 80 cm (32 inches)

TO FIND YOUR CUP SIZE

Measure around the fullest part of your breasts.
If this is the same as your chest size, you need an A cup.
If there is a 2.5 cm (1 inch) difference, you need a B cup.
If there is a 5 cm (2 inch) difference, you need a C cup.

Q Help! I've just noticed weird purple lines on my boobs. What are they?

Stretch marks. When your body grows fast, your skin has to stretch to keep up. Sometimes it hasn't got quite enough elastic and you get these purplish lines. They can happen all over the place – most of us have got some somewhere. There's not a lot you can do to prevent them, but they usually fade over time.

Q Help! I'm 14 and my nipples go in instead of out!

Don't worry – if you've got innies they'll probably grow into outies as you develop. Try drawing them out very gently between your finger and thumb every day until they get the general idea, or you can buy a gadget at the chemist's to do this. However, if your nipples suddenly invert when you're fully developed (from 18), go and see a doctor.

GOOD THINGS ABOUT `BIG` BOOBS

* There's no mistaking you for a man.

* They keep your feet dry.

* You get to play the sexy roles in the school play.

* Boys love big ones.

* Small-bosomed girls are jealous of your curves.

* You've always got somewhere to shove your purse.

* You've got something to put in your bikini top.

GOOD THINGS ABOUT `SMALL` BOOBS

* The best things come in small packages.

* It saves on suntan lotion, if you go topless.

* You get to play Aladdin in the school panto.

* You can go on a trampoline without getting black eyes.

* Boys love little ones.

* Big-bosomed friends are jealous because you don't wobble.

* You look fantastic in sports gear.

27

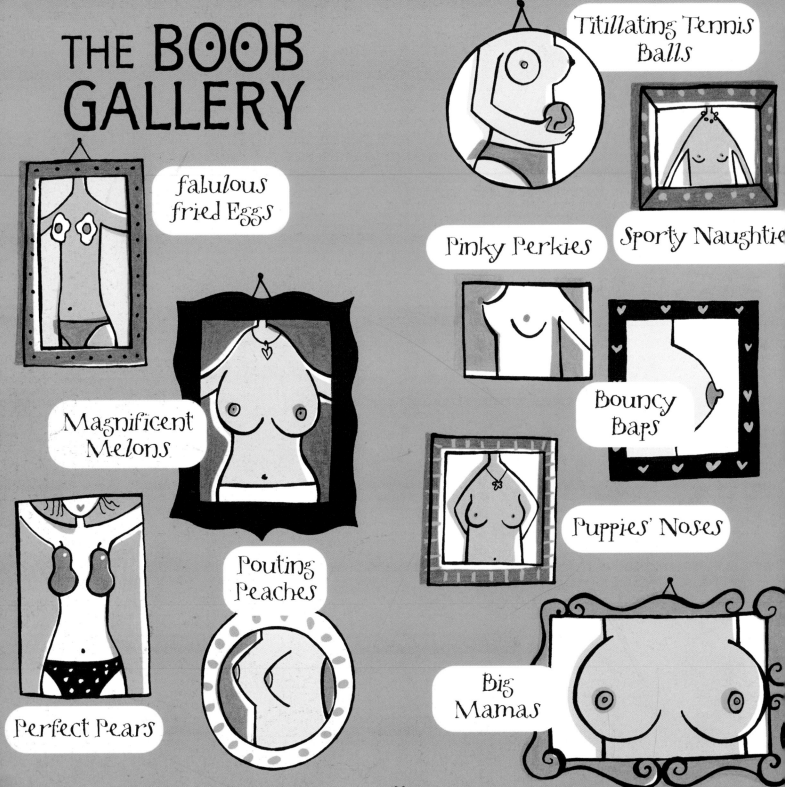

Boob Slang

BAPS

KNOCKERS

TITS

BOSOMS

JUGS

BAZOOKAS

PUPPIES

DUGS

UDDERS

BRISTOLS (cockney rhyming slang: Bristol Cities = Titties)

THREEPENNIES (cockney rhyming slang: Threepenny Bits = Tits)

JUBBLIES

ZEPPELINS

PAPS

Part Three

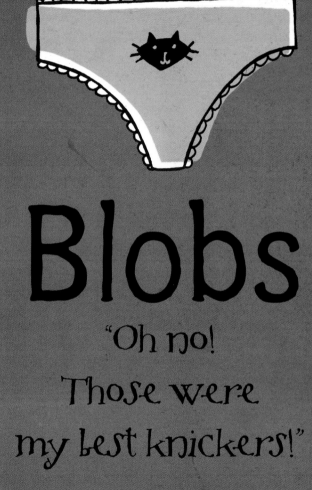

Blobs

"Oh no! Those were my best knickers!"

PERIODS:
What, why, and how to cope without going bright red

Q The girls at school keep talking about periods. What exactly is a period?

Having a period (menstruating) means that every month you lose a small amount of blood through your vagina for a few days. See opposite for a biology lesson!

Q Why do girls have periods and not boys? It isn't fair!

Like it or not, girls are made differently. We can dress like boys, behave like boys, we can even call ourselves Kevin and join the

fire brigade – but there's no escaping the fact that women's bodies are designed to give birth. We don't have to have babies if we don't want to, but isn't it nice to have the choice?

Having periods might seem like a pain in the bum, but it's all part and parcel of being able to start your own family one day.

Q Help! I'm 15 and I haven't started my periods yet. Is there something wrong with me?

Na. Periods can start at any time between the ages of 8 and 17. It usually happens about a year after your breasts develop, but there are no advantages to starting early. If your mum started late, you might too. Also, short, stocky girls tend to come on earlier than tall, thin ones.

WHAT'S GOING ON?

WHY IT HAPPENS: Girls are born with hundreds and thousands of eggs stored in their ovaries. You have two ovaries – one on each side of your uterus (see diagrams). When you reach puberty, sex hormones make the eggs ripen. Every month, an egg is released and takes a one-way ticket to your uterus via the uterine tube. Meanwhile, the uterus lining grows thick and cosy, ready for the egg to arrive. If the egg isn't fertilized (i.e. if you don't get pregnant) the egg and the lining disintegrate and pass out through your vagina with some blood. Voilà: you have a period!

When the bleeding stops, the whole thing starts all over again. This is called your menstrual cycle. (As you can see, this has nothing to do with mountain bikes.)

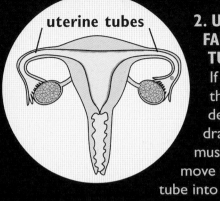

2. UTERINE (OR FALLOPIAN) TUBES:
If the tasselly end of the nearest tube detects an egg, it draws it inside. Tiny muscles and hairs move the egg down the tube into the uterus.

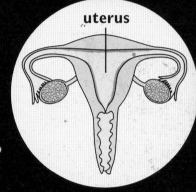

3. UTERUS (WOMB):
Every month, the uterus lining thickens, ready for a fertilized egg to arrive and grow into a baby.

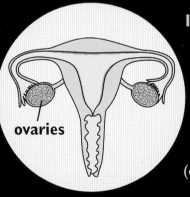

1. OVARIES:
At puberty, hormones make the eggs (ova) in your ovaries ripen. Once a month, an egg is released (ovulation).

4. CERVIX & VAGINA (BIRTH CANAL):
If you don't get pregnant, the uterus lining and egg disintegrate and pass out through the cervix and vagina with some blood (menstrual flow). The cervix has a narrow canal (2 mm) running through it which lets sperm in and menstrual fluid out. It stretches enormously when you give birth.

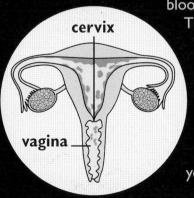

GET THIS!
A single ovum is the size of a full stop.

Q There was some browny-red stuff in my pants when I went to the loo. What could it be?

The chances are, your period is starting. Period blood is often brown instead of red at first.

Q When you have a period, how long do you bleed for and how much blood do you lose?

Most girls bleed for between 3 and 8 days. The average time is 4 days. The flow of blood is usually heaviest at the beginning and lighter towards the end. You usually lose about 2 tablespoons of blood.

Q I haven't started my periods, but sometimes I get a damp patch which dries whitey-yellow in my knickers – what is it?

Around puberty, glands in your vagina start to produce slippery stuff. This helps to keep it clean and lubricated. Some days, you'll hardly notice it, other times it can get quite damp down below. As long as the discharge isn't smelly and you're not sore or itchy, it's nothing to worry about. It's natural, normal and comes out easily in the wash. However, if you'd rather it didn't gum up your gussets or you're worried it'll show during gym, wear a panty liner.

GET THIS!
48% of women bleed for 3–4 days. 35% bleed for 5–6 days. The rest bleed for 7 days or more.

Q Help! I've just started my periods but I don't know whether to use towels or tampons - what's the difference?

Sanitary towels are soft, absorbent pads that you wear inside your pants. They soak up blood as it leaves your body.

Tampons are absorbent plugs (about 6 cm long) that you put inside your vagina. They catch blood before it leaves your body.

Lots of girls use towels when they first start because they're easy to use, but you can use tampons straight away if you like. Or you can mix and match. Some girls prefer to wear tampons in the day and a towel at night - it's up to you. You can often get free samples from magazines - try out different brands to find the one that's best for you.

Q I can't get my tampon in - what am I doing wrong?

Like most things, it takes practice. Next time you have a period, try the tips over the page.

Q I love swimming and I'd like to use tampons, but won't they fall out?

Nice snorkels!

No way - once a tampon is in place, it won't come out until you pull it out by the string. The muscles in your vagina hold it in place.

33

SANITARY TOWELS OR TAMPONS?

SANITARY TOWELS

* They come in different sizes and thicknesses – choose one to suit your shape/the heaviness of your period.

* Press-on towels have a sticky strip on the back. Remove the backing paper and press onto the inside of your pants.

* Change your towel every few hours, even if your flow is light. Blood is perfectly clean, but once it gets outside your body, bacteria can make it smell.

* Don't flush towels down the loo, in case it blocks – bag 'em and bin 'em.

PROs: Easy to use. Effective and comfortable if you choose the right size.

CONs: They can crease or come unstuck. You can't go swimming. Smelly if you don't change them often enough.

TAMPONS

* There are two types: one has an applicator, which guides the tampon into your vagina; the other doesn't – you use your finger.

* Tampons come in different sizes, from mini to super-plus. The bigger the tampon, the more absorbent it is. Choose the right size for your blood flow.

* Once a tampon is inside you, it expands to fit your vagina and prevent any leaks.

* A tampon may leak if it needs changing, in which case you may feel a slight bubbling sensation and the removal cord will be blood-stained.

* Change your tampon at least every 4–6 hours (first thing in the morning if you wear one at night). Leaving them in too long can cause infection – in rare cases it can cause Toxic Shock Syndrome, a serious illness.

* To remove a tampon, you pull it out gently by the cord. You can flush tampons down the loo or bag 'em and bin 'em.

PROs: You can't feel them and they don't show through your clothes. You can go swimming. There's no smell and they're easy to carry because they're so small.

CONs: Some girls have difficulty inserting them. Risk of Toxic Shock Syndrome.

1 Use the smallest tampon you can find (mini-tampons or lites).

2 Wait until your period is heaviest – the tampon slides in easier.

3 Lubricate the rounded end of the tampon (or tampon applicator) with Vaseline or KY jelly and choose one of the following positions...

The Lone Ranger

Straddle the loo with knees slightly bent and hips pushed forward.

Knees up, Mother Brown

Put one foot up on the toilet seat. If that's too low, try the edge of the bath.

The frog

Squat down on the floor over a hand mirror.

Ribbit! Ribbit! Comfortable? Now you need to do a bit of origami.

4 Use your fingers to unfold all the flaps of skin – there's a vagina in there somewhere, it's just a bit shy.

5 Found it? Yay! Now, hold the rounded tip of the tampon (or applicator) at the entrance with one hand. Remember to aim it towards the bottom of your back. Vaginas are built on a backward slope – you can't put a tampon in as if you were sticking a pencil up your nostril.

6 OK, after 3, you're going to gently push the tampon in as far as it will go with the middle finger of your free hand. Ready?

1...2...3...PUSH!

Is it in? If it's in the right position, you won't be able to feel it. If you can, you just haven't pushed it in far enough.

7 If it still won't go in, no worries! Try again next month. Your hymen may still be unbroken, or maybe all you need to do is relax – if you're tense, your muscles will tighten up, making it harder to put the tampon in.

Q I'm sure people can see my sanitary towel when I wear tight clothes. It's so embarrassing - is there anything I can do?

Try using a different brand - some press-on towels are almost as thin as panty liners these days, yet they can be just as absorbent as thicker towels. If your flow is very heavy, try using tampons - they are invisible under the tightest clothes because you wear them internally.

Q My friend says tampons can get lost inside you - is that true?

No, it's physically impossible! Your cervix is in the way and the hole in it is far too tiny for a tampon to go through. The worst that can happen is that you can't find your tampon string - it's almost unknown for them to come off, but very occasionally the string gets tucked up inside your vagina. It's still not a problem - you'll probably be able to find it with your fingers. (It helps if you squat and push as if you were going to the loo.) In the unlikely event that you can't get it out, a nurse or doctor will certainly be able to.

Q I had my first period three months ago. The next month, nothing happened, but now I've come on again - what's happening?

Your hormones are just taking a while to settle down. Periods are often irregular for the first 2 years. Sometimes you have one, then nothing happens for several months. Worrying, feeling ill or just a change of routine (like going on holiday) can also make your periods late or early.

Q My periods are 32 days apart. Shouldn't they come every 28 days?

On average, women have a period every 28 days, but it can vary from 20 to 35.

Q Gran says I shouldn't wash my hair when I have my period – is she right?

In Gran's day, there were all sorts of myths about what you couldn't do when you had a period – for some weird reason, you weren't meant to eat ice cream! In reality, you can do everything you normally do – including swimming, having a bath and washing your hair.

No thanks... It's the wrong time of the month!

GET THIS!
6% of women use no protection at all during their period.

PRIMITIVE BELIEFS ABOUT PERIODS

✺ Shamans used to think menstrual blood was a source of supernatural power.

✺ The Ancient Babylonians thought that a menstruating woman would contaminate everything she touched – if she touched a sack of grain, it was destroyed.

✺ In Ancient Egypt, women had to take special cleansing baths when their periods finished – orthodox Jewish women still follow a similar ritual in a bath called a *mikveh*.

✺ In the Chinese province of Tsinghai, a girl mustn't allow her menstrual blood to touch the earth in case it offends the Earth Spirit. To stop this happening, she is supposed to fasten her trousers to her ankles. (Try doing that in flares!)

✺ In medieval times, it was a sin for a woman to go to church if she was having a period.

✺ In Mediterranean societies, it is traditional to slap a girl's face when she starts her first period, one reason being to bring colour back into her pale cheeks. Ouch!

It can be hard to tell when your first period is due. Some girls get a crampy feeling in their abdomen or lower back, others notice a brownish stain in their pants or spots of watery blood. Some feel weepy or tetchy, but others have no symptoms at all – but don't be scared, be prepared! Here's how:

✿ Wear a panty liner on PE days and public occasions. Period blood doesn't gush out – it trickles through gradually over a few days. A panty liner should spare your blushes until you can get hold of a sanitary towel and freshen up.

✿ Carry change for the sanitary towel machine, a change of pants, a small pack of travel wipes and a press-on sanitary towel in a plastic bag or make-up bag.

✿ If your period starts unexpectedly, go to the nearest loo. Put the grotty knickers in the bag, then freshen up with wipes. Put the press-on towel in the spare knickers and put them on. If you haven't got a towel, a pad of folded tissues or soft loo roll tucked in your pants will work in an emergency.

✿ If you get a little bit of blood on your skirt, try dabbing it out with a paper towel soaked in cold water (hot water will set the stain). Dry under the hand-dryer.

✿ If the stain is really obvious and you're at school, you have three options:
a) Tie your sweatshirt round your waist to cover it up.
b) Ask your mate to blag a change of clothes from Lost Property.
c) Find your favourite teacher and ask for help. (She's trained to deal with these things discreetly.)

Q My friend says it's impossible to get pregnant if you have sex during your period – is she right?

It's all your fault! You got me pregnant!

No! You CAN get pregnant if you have sex during your period. Some girls (maybe you, maybe her) ovulate 2 or 3 days after their periods start, which means there could well be a nice, ripe egg waiting in the wings to be fertilized by the first sperm that pops in to say hello. It's impossible to tell when you're ovulating because your body sometimes pulls a fast one and your cycle changes without warning. The only sure-fire way to avoid pregnancy is not to have sex. Your second best bet is to use a reliable method of contraception every single time – without fail. Run and tell your mate before it's too late!

Q Help! My period pains make me want to go to bed and curl up in a ball.

Now you know why Grandma used to call it "The Curse". Some girls sail through their periods without a twinge but around 80% of us get various aches and pains – it's a hormone thing. The discomfort you can feel is your uterus contracting, due to an excess of prostaglandins. This can cause spasms, abdominal cramp, aching backs and thighs – hardly a barrel of laughs, but rarely anything to worry about. If you feel dizzy, sick, have diarrhoea or a pain that won't go, see a doctor. Otherwise, try these tips...

GET THIS!
The medical name for period pain is dysmenorrhea.

HOW TO MAKE PERIODS LESS OF A PAIN

✳ Ask your mum for some paracetamol or painkillers containing Ibuprofen.

✳ Gently rub your abdomen.

✳ Do some gentle exercises and stretches. This will release endorphins, your body's natural "painkillers", and reduce that bloated, puffy feeling.

✳ Cut out junk food and eat plenty of fruit and veg. A week before, avoid salt, white flour, and caffeine (found in fizzy drinks, tea, coffee and chocolate).

✳ Try herbal teas – mint tea helps to ease cramp; raspberry leaf tea helps to relieve bloating and pains.

✳ Have a warm bath and curl up with a hot-water bottle – heat eases cramp.

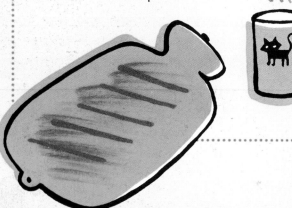

1 Sit on the floor with your legs wide apart. Hold your toes or clasp your ankles. Keep your back straight and breathe in, holding your diaphragm (the muscles under your ribs) up and in. Take a few breaths. As you breathe out for the last time, bend forwards towards the floor.

2 Sit with your knees open and bent to the sides, with the soles of your feet pressed together. Clasp your hands under your toes or hold your ankles. Breathe in deeply, expanding your chest and lifting your diaphragm. Raise your head and feel your stomach expand. Breathe deeply 5 times.

3 Lie on your back with one leg stretched out and pull the other knee up to your chin. Clasp your knee with your arms to ease the strain and hold the posture, relaxing for a few minutes.

4 Stand with your feet apart and move your hips in a full circle – twice in one direction, then twice in the other. Repeat 10 times.

Q Will I have periods for ever and ever?

No. From about the age of 40, you start running out of decent eggs. They don't always mature properly and you don't ovulate as often. The level of your female hormones starts to drop, your periods become fewer, then one day they stop altogether, often when you are around 50. The time when they stop is called the menopause, otherwise known as the change of life. Once you've had the change, you can't get pregnant.

GET THIS!
Woman are the only animals unable to have babies for the whole of their lifetime. In all other species, female animals remain fertile until they die.

Q A few days each month, I turn into the bitch from hell! I'm not usually like this – am I going mad?

Oh no, it sounds like the dreaded PMT (premenstrual tension). It's not an illness as such – it's a truck-load of physical and emotional symptoms that some of us get in the days leading up to our periods. Some girls just feel a bit weepy and tired, others feel horrible, hateful and flip their lids over the slightest thing. No one knows what really causes it, but most experts reckon hormones are to blame.

PMT SYMPTOMS

1 A few days each month, your waistbands are too tight and your bras are too small.
REASON WHY: Either you put them in the boil wash or it's premenstrual fluid retention.

2 Normally he's a babe, but today your boyfriend is so irritating you want to hit him in the nuts with a tea tray.
REASON WHY: Either he really is irritating or you're suffering from premenstrual mood swings.

3 For no good reason, you want to jump off a cliff.
REASON WHY: Either you're into hang-gliding or you have premenstrual blues.

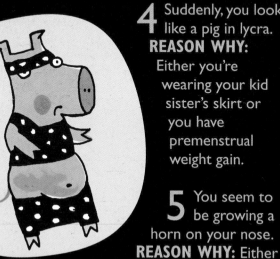

4 Suddenly, you look like a pig in lycra.
REASON WHY: Either you're wearing your kid sister's skirt or you have premenstrual weight gain.

5 You seem to be growing a horn on your nose.
REASON WHY: Either you're a unicorn or you're getting a premenstrual zit.

6 You have just eaten 3 tubes of Pringles, a big, fat cake and a box of chocolate fingers.
REASON WHY: Either you're a hippo and it's your birthday or you have premenstrual carbohydrate cravings.

7 You feel like you've been hit over the head with a tea tray.
REASON WHY: Either your boyfriend is defending himself against you or you have a premenstrual headache.

8 The slightest thing makes you b–b–burst into

wahhhhhhhhh!

REASON WHY: Either you've been watching *Bambi* or you have pre-menstrual weepies.

Q My auntie said she couldn't go swimming because it was the wrong time of the month. What did she mean?

"Wrong time of the month" is another way of saying you're having a period. In the past, it wasn't done to talk about periods, so code words were used instead. Today, most women are much more laid-back about menstruation, but just for fun, here are some expressions you might come across...

✿ Up on blocks.

✿ It's Rag Week.

✿ I've got the painters in.

✿ Red sails in the sunset.

✿ I've got my monthlies.

✿ I've got the Curse.

✿ It's the wrong time of the month.

✿ Arsenal are at home.

✿ Chasing the cotton mouse.

✿ I've got the flags out.

✿ I'm surfing the crimson wave.

SO NOW YOU KNOW...

Now that you know all about big girls' bumpy parts, foldy flaps and furry bits there may be a burning question you're still dying to ask about puberty:

WHY ME?!

OK, it's not just you.
It's every girl who ever walked the planet. There will be good days and bad days, but you mustn't take puberty personally. It's just a sticky in-between stage that happens to everyone. Even the Queen.

It helps to talk about what you're going through. Talk to your friends, your mum or dad, your sisters and grandma. If you can't talk to them and you're worried, speak to an expert. And on sad, mad, paper bag days, remember this: puberty won't last for ever – it's physically impossible!

So ... hang on in there. Go with the flow (period joke – keep your sense of humour!). 'Cos when it's all over, you'll feel like a new woman!

Zitz Glitz & Body Blitz

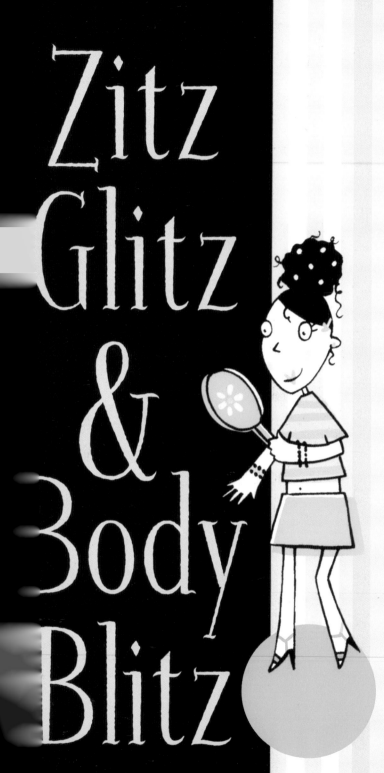

Part four

Body Blitz

"Am I fit or what?"

How to look good, even on bad days!

Oi, Gorgeous! Yes, YOU!

Fed up with seeing images of "perfect" women?

Guess what, they don't exist!
Top models have spotty bums. Pop divas have hairy legs. Even princesses have cellulite – hurrah!
Nobody's perfect.

But there's loads you can do to make sure you look your beautiful best. Like eating the right stuff. Like getting off the couch. Like knowing what suits you. Why bother? Simple! If you look good, you feel good. And if you feel good, you'll be one happy bunny. Here's how...

Q I've got no boobs, stumpy legs and a bum like a football – who's gonna love me with a figure like mine?

Right now, there are hundreds of guys out there who are madly in love with small-bosomed, short girls like you. Having a bum like a football has to be an added bonus – two of their favourite things in one! Don't be fooled into thinking that you have to have legs and boobs like Barbie to be beautiful. You want proof? Next time you're at the shops, look at the women who are part of happy couples. Do they have figures like supermodels? No! They come in all shapes and sizes. You might not think they look beautiful, but their men do! And so will yours.

45

Q *I'm slim everywhere else, but my thighs are like tree trunks. Why?*

Women's shapes vary enormously but there are three basic body types: endomorphs, mesomorphs and ectomorphs. You inherit your body type, so if your mum had crusher thighs, so might you. If you're a mesomorph, it's no good trying to diet your luscious legs away. You may lose a bit of weight but it's more likely to come off somewhere else – like your boobs. If you really want to change your body shape, your best bet is to do exercises that target the area you want to firm up – see page 50.

GET THIS!

The gluteus maximus in the buttock is the biggest muscle in a woman's body.

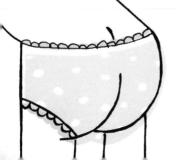

What's My Body Type?

ENDOMORPH: delicate bone structure, short legs, small feet, most likely to gain weight on tum.

MESOMORPH: the classic pear shape – hips larger than shoulders, legs the same length as torso, most likely to gain weight on thighs and bum.

ECTOMORPH: strong bone structure, long legs, does not gain weight easily – if they do, it doesn't all end up in one place.

46

Q Me and my mate look like twins and often wear identical clothes. We're the same size, so why do they always look better on her?

It could be to do with the way she carries herself. Look at the picture and see the huge effect good and bad posture can have on your appearance.

✪ Tammy weighs the same as Tina but looks slimmer because her stomach is pulled in.

✪ The twins are the same bra size, but Tina's bust looks droopy because she hunches over.

✪ Tammy is as shy as Tina, but she looks confident because she keeps her head up.

✪ Tammy is the same height as Tina, but she looks taller because her back is straight.

✪ The twins are the same hip size, but Tina's bum looks bigger because it isn't tucked in.

TAMMY AND TINA THE TWINS   PERFORM THE POSTURE TEST

Tammy:
- head straight
- shoulders down
- level chin
- stomach pulled in
- firm bust
- straight back
- bottom tucked under

Tina:
- head down
- double chin
- rounded shoulders
- droopy bust
- sticky-out stomach
- curved back
- bum sticking out

Q Help! I like PE, but I hate having to get undressed in front of everybody. I'm sure they're all staring at me.

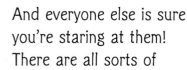

And everyone else is sure you're staring at them! There are all sorts of reasons why we feel embarrassed about our bodies – some girls think they're too fat or too thin, or less developed or more developed than their friends. Others feel shy because they have a skin problem or a scar. We rarely see each other naked, so no wonder we don't know what "normal" bodies are meant to look like. The truth is, although girls' bodies vary enormously, most of these variations are normal. Even so, feeling confident about showing your body is easier said than done. Hopefully, these changing-room tips will help...

Changing-Room Tips

✳ Remember to wear clean, flattering underwear on PE days – baggy or too-tight knickers won't do you any favours.

✳ If you don't wear a bra but you're embarrassed about your budding chest, wear a crop top.

✳ When you get undressed, pull your stomach in – you'll look much slimmer.

✳ If you have to shower, bring a big towel to school so you can cover up completely.

✳ Wear a skirt instead of trousers on PE days so you can pull shorts on underneath.

✳ If you have acne on your back or chest, avoid low-cut swimming costumes.

GET THIS!

The phrase "You can never be too thin or too rich" was coined by The Duchess of Windsor (who was too thin and too rich).

Q *I hate sport, but people keep telling me to exercise. I'm not fat – why should I bother?*

It's rotten having to do something you hate. Many grown women shudder at the memory of being forced to leap after a soggy netball in a freezing playground.

There's not a lot you can do to get out of school sports unless you throw a sickie, but your PE teacher won't fall for that old trick. Everyone needs to exercise to stay healthy, whether they're slim, fat, young or old. But if you're not the sporty type, there are plenty of ways to keep fit which don't involve balls, bats or PE mats. You don't even need to join a gym.

Try and do something active for at least 30 minutes a day. (That's only as long as one episode of your favourite soap!) You don't have to choose a "sport" – just do something to make your heart beat faster that doesn't make you collapse in a sweaty heap. One of the easiest ways to clock up your minimum 30 minutes a day is to walk whenever you can – you don't even have to do it all in one go. Walk to school, take the dog out, use stairs instead of lifts – or go mad and do all three! It'll become a habit you don't even think about.

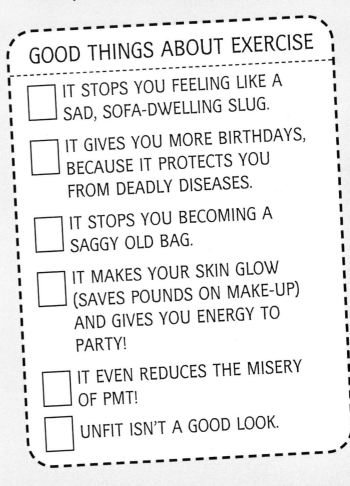

GOOD THINGS ABOUT EXERCISE

- [ ] IT STOPS YOU FEELING LIKE A SAD, SOFA-DWELLING SLUG.
- [ ] IT GIVES YOU MORE BIRTHDAYS, BECAUSE IT PROTECTS YOU FROM DEADLY DISEASES.
- [ ] IT STOPS YOU BECOMING A SAGGY OLD BAG.
- [ ] IT MAKES YOUR SKIN GLOW (SAVES POUNDS ON MAKE-UP) AND GIVES YOU ENERGY TO PARTY!
- [ ] IT EVEN REDUCES THE MISERY OF PMT!
- [ ] UNFIT ISN'T A GOOD LOOK.

BLITZ THAT ANNOYING BODY PART!
Try doing these exercises
three times a week.
(Always remember to warm up first.)

EXER-THIGHSES

The Ballerina

1. Stand with your feet a metre apart. Turn your toes out as far as possible, pointing away from each other. (Heels should be turned in, pointing towards each other.)
2. Keep your shoulders back and your stomach and bum in. Put your hands on your hips.
3. Slowly start to sit, going down as far as you can. Hold for 2 seconds.
4. Slowly come back up and go right up onto your toes, lifting your arms above your head. (Remember to keep your shoulders down.)
5. Repeat 14 times.

Squats

1. Stand with your feet as wide as your shoulders, stomach pulled in, shoulders back.
2. Keeping your back straight, push your bottom out as though you're about to sit down. Go as far as you can and hold for a count of 3.
3. Push your bottom forward and scoop it upwards as you come up.
4. Repeat from the beginning, but this time with your arms stretched straight out in front as you go down. Pull them back as if you are rowing when you stand.
5. Repeat 14 times.

BLUBBERY BUTT BUSTERS

The Stork

1. Stand up straight and pull your stomach in. Without bending your back, stick one leg out straight behind you with the toe pointed. Take it up as far as you can, keeping your leg straight.
2. Repeat 10 times.
3. Change legs and repeat.

Squeezy-bums

You can do this one anywhere – even sitting on a bus (unless it makes you pull funny faces).

1. Either sitting or standing, clench your buttocks together as hard as you can.
2. Hold for a count of three and release.
3. Repeat 10 times.

TERRIFIC TUMMY TONERS

Sit-ups

1. Lie on your back with your knees up and your feet apart, resting on the floor.
2. Put your hands behind your ears, elbows out.
3. Pull your stomach in and sit up as far as you can. (Don't let your chin drop onto your chest – imagine there's an apple under it.)
4. Hold the position for a count of 2, then lower yourself back slowly.
5. Repeat 16 times.

The Plank

1. Lie on your stomach, with your elbows on the floor by your waist and your hands pressed together in front of you.
2. Curl your toes under and lift your bum up so that your knees are off the floor and your back is straight.
3. Supporting your weight on your forearms and toes, suck your stomach in as hard as you can and hold it – imagine you are trying to touch your spine with your belly button.
4. Keep holding it for as long as you can, pulling it in tighter every few seconds ... hold it ... hold it ... hold it...
5. Relax for 30 seconds, then repeat the exercise.

Q I've just bought a skirt to die for, but it's a little tight round the waist. What's the best way to lose a bit of weight?

1 EAT A BALANCED DIET. If you do this you'll get everything you need to stay fit and healthy. Try and eat 5 portions of fruit and vegetables every day. Some foods have more calories than others – e.g. bananas have more than raspberries – but don't get hung up on calories. A banana is better than a doughnut!

2 JACK IN THE JUNK. It's the easiest way to lose weight. You don't have to deny yourself chips and chocolate for ever – just go easy on foods high in fat and sugar. Start reading food labels – some "healthy foods", such as fruit yoghurts, cereals, muesli bars and even tinned peas, contain added sugar.

3 DON'T STARVE YOURSELF. It's unhealthy and it doesn't work. OK, if you cut calories drastically you'll lose weight initially, but you'll put it all back on (plus a bit more, usually) when you start eating normally again. If your body suspects there's a food shortage, it hangs onto its fat reserves – if you try to diet again, you'll find it even harder to lose weight. It's called yo-yo dieting and it can actually make you fatter!

4 GET OFF YOUR BUTT. Apart from the vitamins and minerals you need to stay healthy, food gives you energy. Every time you move, you burn up body fat. Walking burns about 300 calories an hour! The maths is simple:

sofa + junk food x 7 days = unfit, sad person
exercise + healthy food x 7 days = fit, happy person

Q My roommate at ballet school uses laxatives to help her lose weight – is it safe?

No, it's very dangerous. If you use laxatives (tablets that make you poo) too often it can cause dehydration, ruin your kidneys and stop your bowels working. What's more, it's useless as a slimming aid – in the time it takes for laxatives to work, the calories from food have already been absorbed by your body. Any weight you lose is just fluid, and even this is temporary because the body reacts by retaining water, so you feel bloated and can weigh up to 4.5 kg (10 pounds) more.

Some girls take diuretics (tablets that make you pee) to try and lose weight. These are equally dangerous and equally useless – the *only* way to lose weight permanently and safely is to eat a well-balanced diet and do enough exercise.

Q My friend always throws her packed lunch away. I'm sure she has an eating disorder – what should I do?

If someone has an eating disorder, they often do their utmost to hide it from their friends. Some girls say they've already eaten, or wear baggy clothes to disguise their weight loss. Others eat normally in public then vomit or use laxatives in secret. If your friend is obsessed with food and diets and gets angry or upset if you talk to her about it, she may have a problem and need help. If she won't talk to you, tell an adult that you are worried about her and why. She won't thank anyone for helping her right now, but she is in danger of ruining her health and needs expert advice.

What	Why	What to look out for & treatment
ANOREXIA is when a person becomes obsessed with losing weight and deliberately starves themselves.	Often anorexia serves as a way of feeling in control – some girls stop eating because they're afraid of growing up. Others feel pressured into achieving an "ideal" figure.	Anorexics may avoid eating situations, hide food or over-exercise. They may wear baggy clothes to hide their weight loss, and feel anxious or depressed or talk of suicide. Anorexia has adverse effects on health and, in extreme cases, can kill. Treatment may involve going into hospital to stabilize weight. Therapy and medication can help others.
BULIMIA is when someone binges on food then "gets rid of it" shortly afterwards by vomiting or taking laxatives and diuretics (purging).	People with bulimia are usually insecure – they often hate themselves but desperately want to please others. They are rarely overweight, but are convinced they are fat.	Binging and purging are two symptoms to look out for – and these are usually done in secret. Food is comforting, so they binge and then feel ashamed of themselves. Purging makes them feel "back in control". Like anorexia, bulimia can kill, but it can be treated and the sooner someone gets help, the better.
BINGE-EATING DISORDER is when someone eats massive amounts in a very short time (less than 2 hours) until they feel uncomfortably full. If it happens twice a week for more than 6 months, it's a problem.	People who binge-eat are often obese and depressed. They go on diets, get hungry, then binge, or overeat, when they're unhappy or bored.	They may suffer from high blood pressure and are at risk from diabetes, heart disease and other serious illnesses. Binge-eating can be treated, but putting a binge-eater on a diet may make things worse. Some of the treatments used for bulimia work for binge-eaters too, such as cognitive-behavioural therapy. This is where people are taught to understand why they act the way they do and how to stop themselves doing it. Often a combination of therapies helps.
COMPULSIVE OVEREATING is when someone eats non-stop throughout the day and panics if no food is available.	Compulsive-eaters are addicted to food for emotional reasons instead of hunger. It often starts in childhood and happens to people who have never learnt to handle stressful situations. Some make themselves deliberately fat and "unattractive" to avoid dealing with close relationships.	They often suffer from severe weight gain and health problems associated with being overweight. Not all overweight people are compulsive-eaters: compulsive-eaters know their eating pattern is out of control. They may start to lose self-pride, forget to wash or dress properly and feel worthless and lethargic. Compulsive overeating can be cured, and the best treatment includes therapy and nutritional counselling.

POOOH!

You've reached the SMELLY section!

POO-O-E-E!

Q Help! I wash my feet every day, but when I take my trainers off, my feet are minging.

Feet have lots of sweat glands, and when you reach puberty, they can really go into overdrive – especially if they're trapped in trainers all day. If you want toes that smell like a rose, here goes...

HOW TO KEEP YOUR FEET SWEET

1 Wash feet every day and dry carefully between your toes.

2 After washing, use a foot deodorant (powder or spray), or ordinary talc in an emergency.

3 Wear clean socks or tights every day.

4 Avoid nylon socks. Natural fibres like cotton and wool are best – they let your skin breathe, so you get less sweaty.

5 Use special, deodorizing trainer-liners.

6 Don't wear the same pair of shoes two days running.

7 Go barefoot whenever possible.

8 Check for athlete's foot (a fungal infection) or verrucas (foot warts). If you suspect anything, describe it to the chemist or doctor and he'll give you some stuff to treat it.

GET THIS!
6% of girls are born with webbed feet.

9 Use small nail scissors to trim your toenails and cut them straight across so you don't get ingrowing toenails. File any edges but don't file down at the sides.

10 Gently push back your cuticles (the skin growing over the half-moon bit) with your thumbnail after you've had a bath.

Q When should I start using a deodorant?

POOH!

When no one will sit next to you on the bus! Seriously, you should consider wearing an underarm deodorant as soon as you suspect you're sweating more, which is usually around puberty. Fresh sweat doesn't whiff, but sweat trapped inside several layers of clothes rapidly causes BO (body odour). Synthetic fabrics like nylon make the problem worse. If you're not sure whether you need a deodorant (it's not always easy to detect your own smell) ask your mum or your best mate, or if that's too awful, sniff the armpit of your blouse a few hours after you've taken it off. If it smells like an old tomcat, buy an antiperspirant deodorant and get into the habit of using it every day ... please?!

How to avoid BO – it's the pits!

✪ Wash under your arms every day.

✪ Ordinary body sprays don't stop BO. Use an antiperspirant deodorant – this will minimize the amount of sweat you produce and keep you sweet.

✪ Remember to reapply deodorant after you've been swimming or had a shower.

✪ You can buy handy deodorant wipes to keep in your bag for emergencies.

✪ If you prefer, health shops sell anti-perspirant "stones", which keep you fresh without any chemicals.

✪ Roll-on, gel or stick deodorants last longer than sprays.

Worst Case Scenario

HELP! I'm going to a disco in like 5 minutes but my mum forgot to wash my one and only favourite top and the armpits stink!

1 If you have a tumble-dryer, bung in the offending top with a sheet of fabric softener. Or use a dry-cleaning sheet and put it with the top in the bag provided. Let it whizz around for as long as poss – it should take the edge off. (Use the cool cycle if the label says dry-clean only.)

2 Spray the armpits lightly with a fabric freshener, or at a pinch, use one of those ironing sprays and iron it. (Check the label says it's OK to iron your top!)

3 Turn the top inside out and spray the armpits lightly with an aerosol deodorant – it's a last resort, but hey, you're desperate.

4 Never try and cover it up with half a gallon of perfume. You'll end up smelling of too much perfume – and BO!

Q My best friend said I had bad breath. Help!

Don't worry! Everyone – including your best friend – gets halitosis (bad breath) from time to time. It can be easily prevented.

BAD BREATH: THE MAIN CAUSES

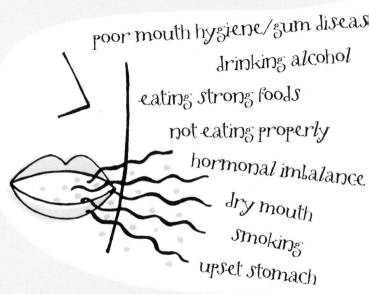

poor mouth hygiene/gum disease
drinking alcohol
eating strong foods
not eating properly
hormonal imbalance
dry mouth
smoking
upset stomach

BAD BREATH: HOW TO CURE IT

★ Go for regular dental check-ups.
★ If the dentist gives you the all-clear, try brushing up on your tooth-cleaning regime.
★ If you need to freshen breath when you're out and about, chew sugar-free gum or carry special breath-fresheners – these come in tablets or sprays.
★ If your bad breath still persists, see a doctor to rule out any stomach disorders.

> Q There's a gang of girls at school and they all smoke. They said if I had a cigarette I could hang out with them – there can't be any harm in having one fag, can there?

It isn't one fag that does the damage, it's getting addicted to them. Wanting to be part of the in-crowd can be really hard to resist, but what if you can't stop smoking? Fag Ash Lil is *not* a great look when you're older (and you *will* get older!). Older smokers don't look glam, they just look desperate – check them out at the bus stop if you don't believe it. Smoker's cough and smelly breath isn't sexy either. Telling you not to smoke will only make you more determined to have a puff, so look at the facts, then decide – it's your life.

SMOKING – THE FACTS

☞ It's against the law to smoke until you're 18.

☞ The nicotine in cigarettes is highly addictive. 99% of teenagers who smoke started by "just having the odd fag".

☞ Cigarette smoking is the major cause of preventable death in this country. Nearly all lung cancer patients are smokers. Smokers are twice as likely to suffer from heart disease and peptic ulcers. Smokers run a far greater risk of developing throat, mouth, oesophageal, pancreatic, kidney, bladder and cervical cancer.

☞ Tobacco stains your teeth, fingers and hair yellow and gives you bad breath.

☞ Smoking turns your skin grey and ages it prematurely, especially the upper lip, which becomes permanently puckered.

☞ Smoking at a young age can scar your lungs, which makes you more likely to get lung disease later in life – even if you quit.

☞ Nicotine poisoning can cause nausea, dizziness and weakness – which is why you feel like puking up when you first smoke.

☞ Smoking is expensive – loads of your spending money will go up in smoke.

☞ Smoking harms the people around you.

Oooh, look – **carrots!**

Q *Help! Every time we go to a party, my mate drinks too much and throws up – I'm really worried about her.*

Most teenagers overdo it once in a while, but you're right to worry. Overdosing on alcohol can be deadly. Around 6,000 15–20-year-olds die every year from alcohol-related causes. If someone who has been drinking passes out or has trouble breathing, get medical help fast – an unconscious person can choke to death on their vomit. It is against the law to buy alcohol if you're under 18, but if you are going to drink alcohol, learn to do it safely.

ALL ABOUT ALCOHOL

The more alcohol a drink contains, the stronger it is. Beer contains around 5%. Wine 9–12%. Spirits 40% or more. Don't mix your drinks – it'll make you feel sick or give you a hangover.

Don't drink on an empty stomach – it'll go straight to your head.

Girls get drunk quicker than blokes after drinking the same amount. We produce less of the enzyme that breaks down alcohol – so don't try and drink your man under the table.

Alcohol dulls your reflexes – that's why you should never get into a car if the driver has been drinking, even if they don't seem or look drunk.

Never walk home on your own if you've had a skinful (drunk girls are vulnerable to muggers/rapists/road accidents). If no one can take you home, call a cab. Any parent would rather pay at the other end than have you dead in a ditch – you'll be grounded, but hey, you'll be alive!

Alcohol relaxes you, but too much can make the coolest person behave like a prat. At best, you'll embarrass yourself. At worst, you'll do something really dumb, like having sex without using contraception.

Pace yourself – if you knock drinks back too quickly, you'll get drunk. Alcohol makes you pee a lot, so it dehydrates you. Drink plenty of water in between drinks and some more before you go to bed to avoid getting a hangover.

If you do drink too much, you may feel dizzy, clammy and sick, and will possibly vomit. Ask a friend to look after you and help you get home.

Q Why should I say "no" to drugs? My mate gets a buzz out of them and feels fine.

Let's be honest. Certain drugs can make you feel good, otherwise no one would take them. But what's also true is that the same drug that makes your mates feel great could make you feel ill, frightened or worse. It's impossible to tell what's in the drug or how strong it is. Even if you only try it once, you're taking a risk – you could overdose or even die. No drugs are 100% safe, and most are illegal.
Check the facts...

Drugs and their effects

What	Effects	Risks and addiction rate
CANNABIS (marijuana, pot, weed, hash, grass, spliff, ganga): Flowers, leaves or resin are smoked in a cigarette (joint), in a water pipe (bong) or eaten in cakes.	Various – from feeling happy and laid-back to tiredness, headaches, paranoia and hunger (the munchies).	Long-term effects are not known, but it can cause memory loss, slowed reflexes, personality changes and may affect your fertility. May cause serious harm to an unborn child. **Low addiction rate.**
INHALANTS: Solvents in paint-thinner, glue, lighter fluid, gas, etc. are sprayed into a bag and sniffed.	Instant buzz, then drowsiness/ sedation. Hallucinations, headache and nausea.	One-time use and overdose can lead to instant death through cardiac arrest/lack of oxygen. Suffocation/choking on vomit. Accidents due to feeling "drunk"/serious burns (many solvents are flammable). **High addiction rate.**
TRANQUILLIZERS (benzodiazepines) (Valium, Rohypnol, etc.): Prescription drugs in the form of tablets, capsules, injections or suppositories.	Calming, relief from tension and anxiety. High doses can make you drowsy and forgetful.	Dangerous if mixed with alcohol. Some tranquillizers cause temporary loss of short-term memory. Risk of panic attacks when trying to quit. Injecting crushed tablets or contents of capsules is very dangerous. **High addiction rate.**

What	Effects	Risks and addiction rate
COCAINE (coke, blow, crack, rock, snow, C): A white powder snorted or injected or smoked. (Crack is a smokable, chemically-altered cocaine.)	Sense of wellbeing, energy, anxiety, panic, reduced appetite. The "high" is followed by a crash.	Easy to overdose, leads to seizures, heart attack, stroke. Repeated use causes paranoia, insomnia and hallucinations. Risk of AIDS and hepatitis from shared needles if injected. **High addiction rate.**
AMPHETAMINE AND METHAMPHETAMINE (speed, meth, crank, crystal, ice, dexies, hearts, whizz, black beauties): Found in diet pills, prescription medicines. Snorted, smoked, swallowed or injected.	Increased energy, alertness, short-lived euphoria.	High risk of overdose, convulsions, coma, death from heart failure, ruptured vessels in brain. Can be fatal if combined with exercise, due to increased body temperature. Risk of AIDS and hepatitis from shared needles if injected. Long-term use: hallucinations, violence, paranoia. **High addiction rate.**
ECSTASY (MDMA) (X, XTC, E): Pills made in illegal labs.	Energy and alertness, happiness, loving feelings.	Serious risk of overdose, heart attack, increased body temperature (causing lethal dehydration), seizures and death, especially when combined with physical activity (dancing, etc.). Long-term use: teeth-clenching, shakes, dry mouth, nausea and cramps, possibly liver and brain damage. **Addiction rate unknown.**
LSD (lysergic acid diethylamide) (acid, trip): A hallucinogenic (distorts sense of time, vision, sound, etc.). Absorbed on paper (blotter) or a sugar cube and chewed. Also tablets/capsules.	Hallucinations, seeing bright colours, out-of-body experiences, ecstatic feeling, sweating, palpitations, nausea.	"Bad trips", convulsions, coma, heart and lung failure, high risk of accidents. Often laced with rat poison, causing brain damage or death. Long-term use: scary visual memories (flashbacks) replayed any time later. **Addiction rate: often causes psychological dependency.**
MAGIC MUSHROOMS: Specific type of mushroom, dried and then eaten whole or mixed in food/drink.	Same as LSD.	Nausea, increased blood pressure, bad trips, mistaking poisonous mushrooms for magic ones. **Low addiction rate.**
HEROIN (smack, mojo, horse, junk, skag): In pure form, a white powder (dried "milk" of opium poppy). Can be smoked or snorted but a more intense high comes from injecting it straight into veins.	Pleasure rush and low sensitivity to pain. Depresses nervous system, causing heart and breathing problems.	High risk of death by overdose, even on first try. Risk of AIDS or hepatitis from shared needles if injected. Runny nose and stomach cramp. Heroin may be laced with quinine/other dangerous substances. **High addiction rate. Withdrawal (cold turkey) is awful.**

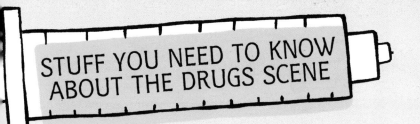

✪ All drugs carry risks – even an overdose of vitamin pills can kill.

✪ Some drugs can kill the first time you use them.

✪ Many drugs are "cut" or mixed with other stuff. There's no way of telling what's in them – could be talc, toilet cleaner or rat poison.

Oh, go on, try it! It's wicked!

✪ Drugs have different effects on different people. A friend may take the same stuff and be OK – you might end up in hospital, or worse.

✪ Drugs are even more risky if you're taking other medication – it can cause a dangerous chemical reaction.

✪ Drugs and alcohol can be a really deadly combo.

✪ Sharing needles is a great way to catch hepatitis and AIDS. Hepatitis can be fatal. There is no cure for AIDS.

✪ Drugs are expensive – if you become addicted, you will have to fund your habit. Unless you're rich, you may have to steal to pay for them.

✪ Drug dealers are criminals – if you become addicted, you'll have to face some seriously scary people who don't give a toss whether you live or die. They may force you to "work" for them if you owe them money – probably as a prostitute.

✪ Coming off addictive drugs can be truly awful.

GET THIS!

The cannabis plant used to be harvested for fibre to make clothes and rope.

The end of the chapter – the start of a NEW YOU?

Are you raring to be toned, honed and glowing with health? What's that? You would take more exercise – only there's something good on telly? You would eat more fruit – but it seems a shame to let this pizza go to waste? OK, so you're only human. There's a time and a place for fast food and chilling out, but not every night of the week, eh? If you want to look your beautiful best (and you know you do), it ain't gonna happen if you're a total slob.

So why not make yourself a little promise? "From now on, I will do at least one healthy thing every day." It could be a big thing, like saying no to fags. Or a little thing, like cutting back on burgers and walking to places instead of calling DadCabs. The more you do, the fitter you'll feel. The fitter you feel, the more fantastic you'll look ... and it won't just be you who notices! Go for it!

You only get one body.

Give it some loving.

Part five

Zits

"Anyone got a paper bag?"

How to make the most of your skin, make-up and hair

Natural beauty...

is a wonderful thing. Some of us are lucky enough to have it, but there are days when nature could do with a helping hand. Or a good slap. Maybe we want to disguise a spot or get rid of a shiny nose. Or maybe we just love playing with glitter and different looks. In either case, it really does help to know your lipstick from your lip wax.

However, true beauty doesn't lie in the bottom of a make-up bag. Lots of girls don't want to wear make-up, so never feel you have to. Fresh skin and healthy hair are really all you need. If your face is a juvenile disgrace and every day is a bad hair day, don't put a paper bag over it! Read on. You SHALL go to the ball!

Q Help! My face looks like a pizza – why am I so spotty?

Lots of people get spots in their teens. When your hormone levels change, your

skin can produce too much sebum (the oily stuff which keeps it soft and waterproof). If that happens, your face looks shiny and your hair follicles may become blocked. If you're lucky, you'll get the odd spot on the end of your nose (always before a party!) and a few blackheads. If you're unlucky, you can end up looking like a target practice with red pustules and fluid-filled cysts – in other words, acne. Spots often get worse just before your period or if you are stressed. They can be painful and embarrassing, but there are things you can do to make them a whole lot better ... read on!

Greasy food gives you spots – FALSE! Chips and chocolate might make you fat, but spots are caused by hormones.

Acne is contagious – FALSE! You can't catch acne off a spotty guy.

You can't inherit acne – FALSE! (Sadly, you can...)

You get spots because you don't wash enough – FALSE! Dirt doesn't cause spots – excess sebum does.

You will grow out of your spots – er ... FALSE! Most people do, but some poor creatures have acne right into their 40s and beyond.

You only get acne on your face – FALSE! You can get it on your neck, back, chest, thighs and – shock horror – on your bum!

HOW TO ZAP ZITS

☐ Don't over-wash or over-cleanse your skin – it makes it even oilier.

☐ Avoid harsh "de-greasing", abrasive or perfumed cleansers and soaps. Find a mild cleanser to suit your skin.

☐ If your skin needs a deep cleanse, use a mud pack (this might make your skin break out, so don't use it the day before a party).

☐ Use a light moisturizer – even oily skin needs moisturizing.

☐ There are lots of different spot creams you can try – don't use too much, though, as they can be very drying.

☐ If things get really bad, go and see your doctor. There are several things you could try that may work, including antibiotics and powerful zit-zapping drugs. You'll need to discuss what is suitable for you.

Worst Case Scenario

I've got a HUGE spot on my chin. I am going on my first date this afternoon. Should I squeeze it?

BIG PUS-FILLED ZIT WITH HEAD

Oh, go on then, but don't make a habit of it. You're not supposed to squeeze spots, as it can spread infection and cause scars if you're not careful. Try and do it the night before if you must, or the spot will "weep" and be difficult to cover up. Here's how:

1 Wash hands and make sure your nails are short or you'll break your skin.

2 Hold a hot wet flannel on the spot for 30 seconds to soften it up.

3 Using a sterile needle, carefully "prick" the head of the spot – just nick the top.

4 Wrap tissues around your fingers and *gently* push the spot from either side until all the pus comes out ... splat! Make sure it's all out or it'll build up again.

5 Dab the spot with antiseptic lotion.

6 If the spot bleeds, put a little piece of tissue on it until it stops, then let the air get to it for as long as possible before using concealer/powder.

BIG RED "BLIND" SPOT

Never squeeze these – they will just get angrier. Cover them! Here's how:

1 Clean the spot and smooth away any crusty bits round the edge.

2 Dab a spot cover stick onto the spot quite heavily in the centre, then tap it into the surrounding skin until it's blended. Don't use liquid foundation – it will slide off and the spot will show by lunchtime.

3 Pat all over your face with all-in-one or powder foundation – be generous!

4 You now look like an explosion in a flour factory, so, using your fat complexion brush, whisk off excess powder for a natural, long-lasting finish.

Q Help! There are so many different types of foundation, I don't know which to use.

If you have normal skin with no spots, you probably don't need foundation – you lucky thing! If you haven't got a perfect complexion, foundation can add colour, even out skin tone, minimize blemishes and work as a base for the rest of your make-up. Find one that suits your skin type and colour. Choose matt for oily skin or moisturized for dry skin.

HOW TO RECOGNIZE YOUR SKIN TYPE

1. Smooth skin, closed pores, matt complexion, occasional spot = NORMAL

2. Rough patches, flaky skin, feels tight after washing, no spots = DRY

3. Shiny "T-zone" with open pores, smooth cheeks = COMBINATION

4. Shine appears soon after cleansing, blackheads, prone to spots = OILY

TYPES OF FOUNDATION:

MOUSSE:
This is light and glides on easily – but it also glides off if you have oily skin. Good for dry or normal skins.

TINTED:
Great for young, dry and blemish-free normal skins – this doesn't do a cover-up job, it just adds a natural glow to your skin. Avoid if you have oily skin, or, like Rudolph, you'll have a very shiny nose.

LIQUID:
This gives light to medium coverage. Good for evening out skin tone but avoid on oily skins. Rubbish at covering spots, as it can slide off or get caked on the crusty bits.

ALL ~IN~ONE:
This comes in solid cream or powder form in a compact with its own sponge. Easy to apply, not too heavy and gives good coverage on all skin types. Used over a spot cover, it is ideal for blemished skin.

STICK/PANCAKE:
Great coverage – best applied with a damp sponge. But unless you're on stage, it can look too heavy on young skins.

POWDER:
Perfect for girls with normal, oily or combo skins who can't get to grips with foundation. Just press onto your skin with a puff for good coverage and a natural matt finish. Brush off any excess with a complexion brush.

Q How do I know which is the right colour foundation?

Always ask for a few testers first. Dab them on your jawline and check them in the daylight. The right colour will disappear into your skin.

Q I look like I've been sunbathing under a sieve. How can I get rid of my freckles?

Freckles are small, flat spots of skin pigment – there is nothing you can do to get rid of them. To stop them getting worse, use a sunblock (it'll stop you getting a tan, though). You can disguise freckles with spot concealer or minimize them with foundation. Just bear in mind that lots of us find freckles really cute – some girls buy special pencils to draw fake ones on!

101, 102, 103, 104....

How to remove make-up

Always remove your make-up before you go to bed or you'll end up with dull skin, puffy eyes and filthy pillows.

BLIMEY – what a night!

1 Remove eye make-up first. If you can't afford a flashy eye make-up remover, good old baby oil works well, even on waterproof mascara. Pour a little onto cotton wool, close eyes and remove with downward strokes, taking care not to drag delicate skin round the eye.

2 Use a mild cleanser to remove foundation and lipstick.

3 Rinse face and pat dry with a clean towel, or use a mild toner to remove any last traces of make-up.

4 Moisturize dry and normal areas, and around eyes. Apply spot treatment to zits.

TOP LIPSTICK TRICKS

Lipstick can light up your face and make you look wonderful – or it can go horribly wrong and make you look like you've had a fight with some jammy toast. To avoid a full-blown lippy disaster, read on...

✪ Vivid, dark or bright lipsticks look too "dolly" on young faces – like a kid who's raided her mum's make-up bag! Go for natural glossy or pearly shades.

✪ Light-coloured lipstick makes your mouth look bigger. Dark lipstick makes thin lips look like slits.

✪ Choosing a shade to suit your clothes or nail varnish often works – that doesn't mean black lipstick with a black dress!

✪ Don't put lippy on cracked lips – eeugh!

✪ To give lipstick more staying power, blot lips with foundation first. Don't go over the edges to make your mouth look bigger – Coco the Clown is not a good look.

✪ Blot excess lippy with a tissue.

✪ Vaseline makes good, cheap lip gloss.

✪ Check for lipstick on your teeth.

✪ Smile! It'll do much more for your looks.

HOW TO CUSTOMIZE YOUR EYES

Eyes are the windows to your soul, or so they say. If it's true, make the most of your windows with these tips.

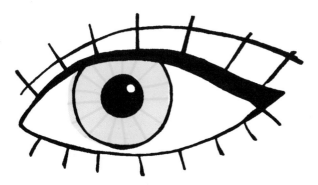

1 Powder eyeshadows stay on better than cream ones.

2 Wear natural colours in the day – it looks right and it's less obvious when they wear off or crease. Dark ones can look really manky by lunchtime.

3 Eye pencils are easier to use than liquid eyeliner. Choose one with a soft texture.

4 Dark eyelashes make eyes look bigger. If yours are pale but you don't like mascara, dye them. You can buy kits or go to a salon. It lasts up to six weeks.

5 If your eyelashes are straight, eyelash-curlers give a wide-awake effect.

Q I'd love to wear nail polish but I always make a mess of it – what's the secret?

You need a steady hand and time for it to dry. You can't rush a nail job, so don't leave it until the last minute, or you'll smudge it. If you're not used to painting your nails, stick to pale, pearly colours – the mistakes don't show as much and they don't look as grotty as dark shades if they chip.

TOP TIPS FOR POLISHED TALONS

✳ Don't use old nail polish – it goes gunky in the bottle really quickly. Get yourself a new bottle of base coat (to stop your nails staining), a coloured polish (to match clothes or lipstick) and a top coat (to prevent chipping).

✳ Give yourself a manicure first – remove old polish, push back any cuticles and file your nails.

✳ Wash and dry hands.

✳ Roll bottle between your palms to mix varnish properly.

✳ Load brush with base coat (but not so it's dripping). The idea is to put a *thin* coat of polish on, not a fat blobby one. Keep your hand steady and quickly stroke the brush from the base to the tip, starting in the middle. Three strokes should do it – one in the middle, two on each side. Don't go over the bit you've just done – it'll pucker.

✳ Paint each nail and wait until dry.

✳ Apply a coat of coloured polish using the three-stroke method and let it dry. You may need a second coat, in which case brush it on and let it dry.

✳ Finish with a top coat, then wait ... wait ... wait ... don't touch anything! Don't stroke the cat or pull your tights up for about an hour. When you think it's dry, dab a finger gently onto your thumbnail to check – if it's tacky, wait some more!

✳ When it's absolutely dry, slap on some hand cream and off you go!

Q Help! I need a new haircut, but I'm scared it'll go wrong.

A great haircut can make you feel like a new woman – but what if it's the *wrong* woman?! Here's how to avoid a cut-astrophe...

No, REALLY, it's all the rage!

1 Get to know your hair... Is it curly, frizzy, straight, spiky or wavy? Is it greasy, dry or normal? Is it thick, fine, limp, flyaway or coarse? What do you dislike about it? Too long? Too short? Too difficult to manage? Too young? Too old-fashioned?

2 Find a new look... Tie your hair back and look at the shape of your face in a mirror. Is it round, square, heart-shaped, long, thin or oval? Find a pile of magazines and pull out pictures of models with similar face shapes to yours. Cut out and keep the ones with haircuts that you like.

3 Think about whether the haircut you're after suits your lifestyle. Is it worth spending hours blow-drying a "do" that's going to spend its time in a swimming pool?

4 Can you afford to go to the hairdresser's every six weeks? Short, precise cuts need regular trims to keep them in shape.

5 Find a brilliant hairdresser – if one of your mates has a great haircut, find out where she had it done and make an appointment for a consultation. It's usually free and it's your chance to discuss the kind of look you want with the stylist. Take your magazine pictures with you but don't set your heart on having an identical cut.

6 If you liked the stylist, if her suggestions were good ones and if you felt she listened to you, book in!

7 Take someone you trust to keep you company and give you support.

Q How do I get rid of dandruff?

Dandruff isn't catching, but snowy shoulders aren't cool. Flaky bits can be caused by not rinsing properly, a build-up of styling products or a dry scalp. Real dandruff is caused by a microbe which speeds up skin-shedding. It can happen if you're run-down, have an allergy or if your hormones are going loco. Ask your chemist for a treatment shampoo – it should knock your dandruff on the head in about 3 weeks. If it doesn't, see your doctor – you may have eczema or psoriasis, which she can treat in other ways.

Q I hate my curls! How can I get rid of them?

Why are none of us happy with what we've been given? It's nature's way of letting us play hairdressers, of course! If you want straight, sleek hair, there are loads of electric hair-straighteners around that do a great temporary job. Permanent hair-straightening involves chemicals that break down the structure of your hair. It lasts for ages but can make your hair brittle.

Q I hate having straight hair – how can I make it curly?

Try some of these temporary tricks to see if Curls R U, and if you love the look, you could go for something more permanent – like a perm!

HOW TO CURL UP FOR THE NIGHT

Benders

Rollers/ heated rollers

Perming

Spray

Curling tongs

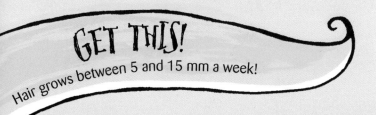

GET THIS!

Hair grows between 5 and 15 mm a week!

HAVING A BAD HAIR DAY?

The only people who don't have bad hair days are bald. Hair that won't do as it's told can be caused by all sorts of things:

- ✪ Static electricity in the air
- ✪ Lying in a strange position
- ✪ Someone putting a curse on you
- ✪ Change in diet
- ✪ Illness
- ✪ Hormones
- ✪ Using different shampoo/conditioner
- ✪ The weather
- ✪ Washing in different water (e.g. if you go on holiday, the water may be harder/softer)
- ✪ Nylon pillowcases

It must have been my pillowcase...

GET A GRIP

Laugh in the face of bad hair days by getting a grip, some slides and some hair bands, etc. Pin, plait, twist, bead or braid your hair into place. Show it who's boss – and if all else fails, get a hat!

WHICH HAIRBRUSH?

TYPE	PROS & CONS
Small, round brush	Good for making tight curls.
Semi-circular brush	Good for creating bounce rather than waves when blow-drying.
Natural bristle brush	Grips hair well for styling but can break it – be gentle.
Synthetic bristle brush	Hairdressers prefer this type – gentle on wet hair and easy to clean. Can slip slightly when styling.
Round-tipped brush	Good for brushing wet hair and for sore scalps, as it doesn't scratch.

GET THIS!
You lose about 80 hairs a day.

Worst Case Scenario

Help! I only washed my hair yesterday but it's gone greasy and I haven't got time to wash it again.

If you can get to a chemist, buy one of those puff-in, brush-out shampoos – it'll absorb the oil and make your hair look and smell fresh in an instant. If you can't get hold of any dry shampoo, use talcum powder. Don't shake it too hard or you'll end up looking like a spook – just sprinkle a little bit onto your scalp, massage it in gently, leave for a few minutes, then brush it out.

If you've got dark hair, dry shampoo can make you look a bit dusty, so try this:
1. Add a teaspoon of strained lemon or lime juice to half a cup of warm water.
2. Use a cotton-wool ball and dab the mixture over your scalp to absorb the grease – it'll bring back the shine, too.

Q I want to get my ears pierced – will it hurt?

Not much and only for a second – it just feels like a hard pinch. Don't let your mate do it with the compasses out of your maths set – go to a reputable salon or big department store.

Err, shouldn't you wash them...?

Most use an ear-piercing gun – a stapling device which "shoots" a stud earring through your lobe. You need to keep the earring in or the hole will close up. Twist it regularly and keep it clean with surgical spirit. Oh, and don't wear hoops for PE – if they get caught, you'll rip your ear lobe.

Q I want to get a tattoo but my mum says I've got to wait until I'm 16 – why is she being so boring?

Most reputable tattoo parlours won't take you on unless you're over 16. You can lie about your age, but before you take the plunge, think carefully about the following – for your *own* sake.

♥ It's permanent! It might fade a little, but it will never wash off. It can sometimes be removed with lasers, but don't bank on it. Why not try a non-permanent tattoo first?

♥ It hurts! To create a design, insoluble dye is injected beneath your skin with a needle. Having a design on your lower back is particularly painful.

♥ A cute little fish on your tummy will turn into a big fat whale if you get pregnant – and it'll turn into a wrinkly whale when you're an old lady.

♥ When you get older, other people might judge you by your tattoo.

♥ Whatever you do, make sure you go to a reputable parlour and that they use a new, sterile needle on you – a contaminated needle could give you hepatitis or AIDS.

Part Six

Glitz

"Does my bum look big in this?"

We get to the bottom of your style problems

Q What should I wear to make me look taller and slimmer?

Stilts and a tent? No really, there are lots of tried-and-tested tricks that can make you look taller and a whole dress-size smaller...

WEAR DARK COLOURS: Black, grey, dark green, navy, brown and deep purple make you look instantly slimmer. White trousers will never, ever disguise a lardy bum. And pale pink or fawn just make you look naked.

WEAR ONE COLOUR ALL OVER: Mixing colours can chop you in half and make you look chunky.

WEAR BIG, IRREGULAR PATTERNS: These make large areas look smaller.

WEAR THIN, VERTICAL STRIPES: These make you look extra-willowy. Avoid horizontal stripes – they would even make a stick insect look chubby.

WEAR SLIGHTLY FITTED STUFF: If you're short and large, you'll look a million times lovelier in clothes with a bit of shape to them. Don't wear clingy stuff – it just screams, "Hey, here's my fat bit!" Instead, buy clothes that skim *over* your squishy bits.

WEAR MATT FABRICS: Shiny, floaty, glittery fabric shouts, "Whey-hey! Look at this!" Only use it to draw attention to your best features – fab shoulders, great bosoms, a tiny waist, etc.

WEAR THE RIGHT SKIRT LENGTH: If you've got mini-legs, maxi-skirts will drown you. Go for something that ends around the knee or higher if you've got slim pins.

WEAR WELL-FITTING TROUSERS: For max skinniness and height, wear well-fitting (never skin-tight) trousers that skim your body. Check they're not too tight around the waist or you'll squish over the sides!

Q I look like a beanpole – I've got no curves. Help!

If you stand still long enough, you'll probably get booked by Models One. It's fashionable to look like you – tough on the rest of us, but if that's no comfort and you want more curves, here's what to do.

✪ Wear a padded bra.

✪ Wear light, bright colours – hot pinks, metallics and mad patterns.

✪ Wear woolly, patterned tights – stripy ones add loads of curves.

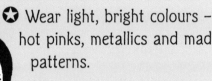

✪ Wear chunky knits, layers, textured material, fake fur, anything fluffy or ruffled.

✪ Avoid wearing one dark colour all over – you'll look lanky.

✪ Anything flared will make you look curvier, so flared jeans and flared skirts are good – long pencil skirts make you look like ... a long pencil.

Q Help! The gusset of my tights always ends up round my knees.

Wrong size, baby! Tights are usually sold in small, medium and large, but unfortunately, different brands measure up differently. Here are some tight dilemmas and solutions.

The half mast
The legs are too short. Try another brand that gives a height guide.

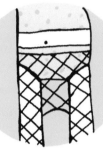

The stranglehold

The legs fit, but the waist's too tight. In an emergency, cut a little v-shape in the elastic at the sides – don't cut as far as the actual tights or they'll run. In future, try tights with a "comfort waistband".

The twist
Feels like one leg is on backwards? Take them off and start again. Make sure they are round the right way and ease them up slowly.

Q My boobs look really small, even in a padded bra – how can I make them look bigger?

Try wearing clingy tops, horizontal stripes, light colours and shiny fabric – these draw attention to what you've got. Avoid low-cut tops – high necklines make your bosoms look bigger. Make your waist look as small as possible by wearing wide, stretchy belts. This gives the illusion that you've got more up top than you really have. Dresses with darts will take the material in under your bust and make the most of your curves.

I can't
BREATHE!!!

Q I've got massive bosoms – how can I make them look smaller?

Oh, be quiet! You look fantastic and you know it. Sorry – just jealous! If you don't want to look like a Big Girl's Blouse, stick to dark colours. Avoid clingy, lycra tops and skimpy woollies – you'll look like you've shoplifted melons. Don't wear really low or high necklines – a modest V-neck will minimize your bust. Avoid shiny fabric, frills, ruffles and jewellery that draws attention to your cleavage. Wear single-breasted jackets – double-breasted ones will make you look as if you've got one huge boob.

Q My arms are so long that my handbag drags on the pavement. How can I make them look shorter?

Join a group of orang-utans? Failing that, you can disguise long arms by wearing three-quarter length sleeves or by pushing your long sleeves up to just below the elbow. Simple, but it works.

Q Help – my tights have got a *ladder* and I haven't got a *spare pair.*

Don't panic. You can stop the ladder getting worse by rubbing it with soap or painting it with clear nail varnish. If the ladder is in a really visible place, like on the top of your foot, wear your tights backwards.

HOW NOT TO LOOK PANTS IN KNICKERS

No matter how fab the outfit, the wrong pants make you look daft. Here are some classic Pants Faux Pas.

VPL (Visible Panty Line)
CAUSE: Pants too tight in the leg/the wrong shape for tight trousers or skirts.
CURE: Wear short-shaped briefs or a thong.

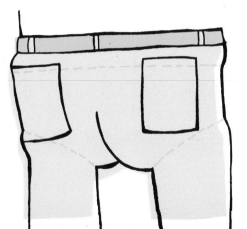

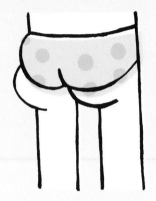

Two-faced Cheek
(pants up crack, creating four buttocks)
CAUSE: Pants badly cut or wrong shape for your bum.
CURE: Try a style that won't cut your buttocks in half – a thong, trouser-pants or briefs with lower-cut legs.

Seamy Sides (seams showing through tight clothing)
CAUSE: Frilly or seamed knickers showing through clothes.
CURE: Smooth, seamless knickers.

Dark Side of the Moon
CAUSE: Dark-coloured knickers under a light skirt.
CURE: Wear flesh-coloured knickers – or a slip (if you're over 50!).

WARNING
Never go knickerless in tights unless they have a cotton-lined gusset – your pubes will go static and you'll get pimples on your bum!

Q Help! I've got a wardrobe full of clothes but nothing looks right.

Everybody suffers from wardrophobia now and then – that awful moment when you realize the fake fur trousers that looked so cool in the changing-room actually make you look like a pantomime horse. As you look in the mirror, you realize why those Lurex leggings were half price – no one else would be seen dead in them! Tired of being a fashion victim? The best way forward is to study these common mistakes and avoid them like the plague.

1 Never shop with a tart, or a slob, or anyone else whose idea of fashion is wildly different from yours. They will try and get you to dress how they dress, and you may not look so good in rubber or pie-crust collars.

2 Don't buy the latest fashion if it doesn't suit you. Obvious, but it's a trap we all fall into. If mini-skirts are in and they're not for you, it doesn't mean you're doomed to wear maxis. If you have thunder-thighs, just compromise – wear shorter skirts, not knicker-pelmets!

3 Check it from every angle: Does your bum look big? Can you sit down without showing your pants? Will your bra-straps show? Is it see-through? Can you walk in it? Does it squash your boobs? Is the fabric cheap and nasty? If so, don't go there!

4 If you don't love it, leave it. If you love the style but hate the colour, leave it – you'll never learn to like it. If it almost fits, leave it – you'll probably never shrink. If it's a bit too short, leeeeave it – it'll never grow.

7 Don't try and guess if the new top will match the skirt at home – if you're buying separates to go with something, bring the other item with you in a bag or wear it to the shops.

8 Don't squeeze into a size smaller in the thin hope you'll lose weight. Always buy the right size – who's gonna check the label? You'll look much better in the right fit and you can wear it now!

5 What works on the catwalk won't always work in real life. Before you buy anything extraordinary, ask yourself when and where you are going to wear it. Clothes made from space-age plastic are noisy, sweaty and uncomfortable. Sky-high platforms are akin to walking with paving-slabs strapped to your feet – avoid if you live on a hill, etc., etc.

6 Don't leave without trying it on: dress sizes vary enormously from shop to shop. Most shops will exchange, but it's a wasted bus fare and you'll need the receipt.

9 Choose colours that suit you. Some of us look fab in black – others look like the living dead. It all depends on your skin tone and hair colour. You either have yellow, pink or blue skin tones. If you're not sure, ask at the make-up counter. If you're yellow-toned, avoid yellowy colours (i.e. orange, mustard). If you're pink, strong pinks/scarlets can make you look lobstery. And if you're blue, avoid overly-blue stuff or you'll look kind of frozen!

Q My mum insists on taking me to a kids' shoe shop to get my feet measured - why does she have to show me up like this?

She does it to get you back for ruining her figure when you were born. Na, she doesn't really - if you're under 21, she does it because your feet are still growing. If you wear badly-fitting shoes now, you'll end up with corns, bunions and gross, painful trotters by the time you're her age. Go in disguise, get your feet measured, then in a calm, mature way, pick out which shoes you like.

Oooh, darling, those bows are so you!

Q Help! I've got massive feet - what shoes should I wear?

Dear Bigfoot, whatever you do, avoid white or your feet will look like ocean liners. Stick to black, brown and neutral colours. Elongated pointy shoes and fat platties are a no-no – go for square toes. Flatties can make your foot look bigger – choose a medium heel which gives the illusion of a smaller foot.

Q Help! New shoes always rub my heels to bits at the back!

Go to the chemist, find the foot counter and look for special, heel-shaped plasters that prevent blisters. Wear them to protect your heel until your shoes soften up with wear, and never pop yer blisters – they might get infected.

Q Help – I've got short legs but I'm not allowed to wear heels to school.

If you want to make your legs look longer, tottering heels aren't the answer. They just push your feet forward, squash your toes and make you look like a short kid in big sister's shoes. The trick is to find shoes with a medium heel and a thicker sole, or shoes cut low at the front – this style makes legs look longer as if by magic.

Wow! It's easy to see who's been reading this book. They smell good. They look fit. And they dress like a dream. If that's not you yet, it could be! Try doing it one step at a time.

There are some things you can change instantly – like personal hygiene and posture. Other things take longer, like noticing the benefit of eating the right food and exercising – but you'll soon notice the difference, so keep it up.

Dress sense also develops over time. Style isn't to do with how big your clothes allowance is – it's about finding out who you are and what works best for you. So have fun – experiment!

Remember, some things that bug you about your body will get better all by themselves – you haven't finished growing yet! Of course, there are some things you just can't change. But hey, learn to love your big nose and chubby thighs. There are loads of small-nosed, weedy-thighed girls who would love to look like you! Why? Because you are the most beautiful girl in the world.

Believe it and you will be!

Snogs, Sex & Soulmates

Part Seven

Soulmates

'Cos a girl's best friend isn't always a diamond.

WHAT ARE FRIENDS FOR?

Oh, please! They're dancing AGAIN!

There comes a time in every girl's life when she realizes that while her aged parents offer a fantastic taxi service, their taste in music sucks, their idea of a good night out is a dull night in and they look sad when they dance. This is why we need mates. Friends v. Parents? No contest!

What parents say	What friends say
You can't go out looking like that!	Love that miniskirt with those thigh boots!
Call this music?	Man, these lyrics are so deep.
Put a coat on – it's snowing.	Why bother wearing spaghetti straps if no one's going to see them?
What time do you call this?	What? It's only 3 in the morning!
Let's go to the zoo!	Let's go skinny-dipping in the boys' pool.
You can't possibly walk in those!	5-inch stilettos! Can I borrow them, *pleease*?
Take that muck off your face!	Great lippy!
Have you finished your homework?	Have you finished with your bloke?
You treat this place like a hotel.	Everybody round to my place!
Would you like some lemonade?	Vodka and cherryade, anyone?
All you do is watch the telly.	Come round and watch the vid of us at that party we crashed.
That's not good for you!	Have you got a light, mate?

Q Help! I'm confused – I don't know who I am, what I want or who to hang out with any more.

When you were little, you just wanted to be a princess – life was so simple! Then you grew up. Now your body and mind keep changing and it can feel like you don't know "you" any more. To make things harder, everyone else is telling you what to do, what to think and even what to wear. But hang on – this is your personality, not theirs! The "true you" is a unique combo of different things that are constantly changing. A good way of finding out what makes you tick is to experiment. Change your hair, try new activities. Go to new places and meet new people – you've got your whole lifetime to discover yourself.

some stuff that makes you YOU.

looks

likes

talents

ambitions

1. Your looks
2. Your style
3. Your likes and dislikes
4. Your beliefs
5. Your interests
6. Your talents and weaknesses
7. Your voice and the things you say
8. Your sense of humour
9. How you treat people
10. Your ambitions

GET THIS!

"Friendship with oneself is all-important because without it, one cannot be friends with anyone else in the world." (Eleanor Roosevelt)

Q Help! I've got blonde hair – everyone assumes I'm dumb.

It isn't just clothes that come with labels – it's people too. We're all guilty of judging each other on appearance. Great if your label says "Intelligent superbabe", but a real bummer if it's screaming "Blonde bimbo" just because of your hair colour. There are loads of dumb assumptions people make without bothering to get to know you. Why? They're basically ignorant, jealous ... or just rude. It's embarrassing and hurtful, but don't take it personally – it says more about them than it does about you.

Labels you should ignore:

GIRLS WHO WEAR GLASSES: geek, swot, goody-goody

PRETTY GIRLS: thick, vain, shallow

GIRLS WHO AREN'T INTERESTED IN BOYS, MAKE-UP AND CLOTHES: dyke, butch

GIRLS WHO ARE BIG: stupid, greedy, lazy

GIRLS WHO ARE VERY SLIM: anorexic, neurotic

GIRLS WITH BIG BOOBS: slut, flirt, freak

GIRLS WHO DRESS DIFFERENTLY: weirdo, loser

What to do if you've been wrongly labelled:

1. Don't bottle it up. Talking to girls in a similar situation might give you some tips.

2. Learn how to deal with your reaction to stupid comments. Anyone who says nasty things clearly has a problem – pity them!

3. Educate people – they may be using words that are offensive now, but weren't in the past. Explain what you prefer to be called, politely but firmly.

4. Don't "become" your label by believing in a nasty comment made years ago. Make a list of all your good points and hold on to positive feelings about yourself.

Q Help! I'd like to make new friends but I'm really shy.

There's nothing worse than thinking you are going to make a complete dork of yourself in public; going bright red, not knowing what to say, saying the wrong thing or being rejected are things we all dread. Shyness can be conquered, though – here are some ways:

1 Imagine you've known the person you're talking to for years.

2 Smile! You'll look friendly and approachable, even if you're shaking in your stilettos.

3 If you have to walk into a room full of people, imagine they're sitting on the loo – they'll seem far less scary.

4 Plan what to say in advance. Find out what people are into. If it's horses, don't say "Do you like horses?", in case they just nod. Say "You know lots about horses... Could I ask you something about them?"

5 Remember that everyone isn't looking at you – you're not the Queen.

6 If you're not a great talker, be a great listener. Show you're interested by asking questions: "Really? Then what happened?"

7 Look confident – chin up, shoulders relaxed, back straight. Look people in the eye, and if your hands are shaking, put them behind your back.

8 Keep saying "I'm in charge!" to yourself, like you're the boss. After all, why should you feel inferior to the other person?

9 If someone says "hi", don't just say "hi" back – offer them a chip, ask if they want to join in, pay them a compliment... Anything to show you want to be friends.

10 Join in! Do activities where you'll meet people who are into the same stuff – that's when friendships happen naturally.

IT TAKES ALL SORTS

Some girls like to hang out in a crowd, some like to have one best friend and others prefer to pic 'n' mix. While each friend is unique, they tend to fit certain categories – so where do your mates fit in?

BESTEST MATE: You're soul-sisters who like the same things. You're so close, you tell each other everything – including the truth!

OLD CHUMS: You go way back! You were both sheep in the school nativity. You don't see each other much, but when you do, it's like you've never been apart.

PONY PALS/BALLET BUDDIES: Friends who share the same activities. When you are together you're as close as anything, but you don't go out of your way to meet up.

FAKE FRIENDS: They look like sweet mermaids but they're fishing for something and just pretend to like you till they get it. Avoid!

MUM'S MATE: A girl your mum thinks you should invite over for tea ... but why? (You don't tell *her* who to play with!)

DIVA: Leader of the in-crowd. You only hang out with her to make yourself look cool. Everyone's scared of her, but deep down she's a bit sad – she's got no real mates.

GIRL PACK: These are the girls you call on when your bezzy mate has fallen out with you or been grounded. You like each other lots and hang out at school in a boy-scaring bunch.

FAIR-WEATHER FRIEND: This girl just wants to have fun. She'll share the good times, but if you're having a bad time, you won't see her for dust.

MONA-LENA: A walking crisis, she has to lean on people or she falls over. If you have the patience to adopt her, you'll be rewarded with puppy-like affection.

Q Help! My so-called best mate told me I had BO – should I forgive her?

Depends how she told you. If she climbed on the school roof and shouted it through a megaphone, cross her off your Christmas card list now! If, however, she took you aside and whispered, "Listen, mate – not sure your deodorant's working properly," she's done you a favour. Say thanks. Surely it's better to hear the truth from your best friend rather than go round minging? It might have hurt, but she has your best interests at heart.

Good Mates OR... Bad Mates?

Good Mates	Bad Mates?
Good mates don't mind you having boyfriends.	Bad mates have your boyfriends.
Good mates keep secrets.	Bad mates spread gossip.
Good mates let you cry.	Bad mates make you cry.
Good mates help you up.	Bad mates let you down.
Good mates let you go first.	Bad mates let you go.
Good mates listen.	Bad mates are too busy talking.
Good mates laugh with you.	Bad mates laugh at you.
Good mates say sorry.	Bad mates forgive no one.
Good mates are giving.	Bad mates only take.
Good mates stick together.	Bad mates tear you apart.

It's my last one but YOU can have it.

Blah blah blah... Did you say something?

89

Q Help! My parents don't like my friends - what can I do?

Parents always fear the worst - it's their job. When you refuse to bring your mates home, they naturally assume you must be hanging out with hookers or hooligans. If you don't tell them all the good things about your friends, parents are forced to make snap judgements about them based on brief, doorstep encounters. Little wonder they leap to the wrong conclusions. Try seeing it from their point of view, then put them straight. This is what your charming, intelligent friends look like from where Mum and Dad are standing:

What your parents see:

Long black hair + long black clothes + Doc Martens = KATIE WORSHIPS SATAN

Sexy clothes + make-up + heels = MANDY IS A SLUT, AN UNMARRIED MOTHER

Pale skin + slim and grungy = KARA'S A DRUG ADDICT LIVING IN A SQUAT

Cool boy + bling + money = KELVIN IS A DRUG DEALER, PIMP

What they're really like:

Katie is a blood donor. Her mum works as a costumier and makes all her clothes.

Mandy's a cheerleader. She's raised loads for the Children's Hospital.

Kara's a dancer - she's just got a grant for the Russian Ballet School.

Kelvin got 98% in Humanities and wants to be a vicar like his dad.

Sadly, although we'd love to be friends for ever, it isn't always the case. Friends fall out. Or they move away. Hardest of all to bear is when a friend dies. It's only natural to be sad, to miss them and to think that life will never be as good again. But remember, although no one can ever replace your friend, the world is full of potential new best mates, all with their own lovable ways. When you find each other – and she or he could be just round the corner – the friend you've lost will become a wonderful memory.

You'll never forget her, but one day you'll find yourself feeling happy thinking about the good times you had together, and the awful hurt will fade.

Part Eight

Sex & Snogs

What's really going on in boys' brains (and down their boxers!)

Q How come girls have such a tough time growing up and boys don't?

But they do! Boys might not have to worry about their bra size or the price of tampons, but they've got plenty of other reasons to get their boxers in a twist. Lots of weird mind and body stuff is happening to them too. If anything, it's harder for them because they'd rather be skinned alive than discuss personal problems with their mates. They suffer alone. So if you see one, be gentle – chances are, he's having an even worse time than you.

THINGS BOYS WORRY ABOUT

Their voices breaking

Being spotty and smelly

Their weight

Their height

Embarrassing erections

Sex – doing it wrong, not doing it at all, having no one to do it with

Crying in public

The size of their willy

Being a loser

Nobody fancying them

Not being cool

Being bullied

Not fitting in

Being laughed at by girls

Being gay

Screwing up in front of their mates

Being crap at sport

HOW BOYS CHANGE AT PUBERTY

Boys usually hit puberty when they're about 13, but it can begin any time between 10 and 18. It starts when a hormone called testosterone is released into their bodies – this kick-starts their testicles into making sperm and triggers off all sorts of changes that will eventually turn them into fully-fledged blokes.

1 THEY GROW TALLER (so they can get rude magazines off the top shelf).

2 FACE SHAPE ALTERS (so they look old enough to get into X-rated movies).

face shape alters

moustache

taller

deeper voice

3 MOUSTACHE AND BEARD BEGIN TO GROW (so they nick your razor).

4 VOICE GETS DEEPER (so they can get out of choir).

5 SHOULDERS AND CHEST GET BROADER (so they can carry your shopping).

6 PUBIC HAIR AND UNDERARM HAIR GROWS (so how come they never wax?).

7 PENIS AND TESTICLES GET BIGGER (so they fill their boxers).

8 SPERM IS MADE IN TESTICLES (so they can make babies – watch out!).

beard

broader chest

hair grows

GET THIS!
On average, boys reach puberty later than girls.

Q Which planet do boys come from?

It has been said that we're from Venus and they're from Mars, but boys aren't aliens really. Once you get to know them, you'll find they're human after all. Here are some of the exciting varieties:

1. **FOOTY FAN:** He lives for Match of the Day. If you stood stark naked in front of the telly he'd tell you to move in case he missed a goal. His team is his tribe.

2. **JOHNNY REBEL:** He's cool, he's mean, he's moody. Very moody – it's like PMT! If only he wasn't so good-looking...

3. **CLASS CLOWN:** If you fancy this one, your best bet is to laugh at his jokes. Don't tell your own or he'll walk off the stage.

4. **ARTY FARTY:** A deep thinker who deeply thinks he's misunderstood. Nobody understands him, so don't even try.

5. **BOY NEXT DOOR:** You used to play in his paddling pool as kids. But somewhere along the line, he turned into Brad Pitt!

6. **MR POPULAR:** Cute but cool. Mature and very clever – he'll be a sexy lawyer or a doctor one day. Hard to get to, this one.

7. **SHY GUY:** He might be seriously lush but he's already decided you'll reject him, so you have to make the first move.

8. **GEEK:** His head's always in a book, but somehow his weird genius turns you on. If you want him, you'll have to swot up.

9. **ACTION MAN:** First you have to catch him! Put on your PE kit and knock his sports sox off!

10. **CAMP DAVID:** He acts gay but probably isn't. Who cares? – a man who actively begs you to come shopping!

Q Help! I get on really well with this lad from school, but when he's with his mates he just blanks me.

When boys are with their friends, they turn into different people (or animals). This is perfectly normal, and once you understand it you'll stop taking it personally.

Why boys behave like gorillas when they're with their mates

⭐ They love to be part of a gang – it's to do with hunting woolly mammoths together during prehistoric times.

⭐ They are secretly scared of girls – they haven't sussed us out yet.

⭐ Boys get the mick taken if they admit to liking a girl – which is why they diss you in front of their mates. When the leader gets a girlfriend then suddenly it's OK to have a relationship.

⭐ Boys hate to lose at anything – which is why they go ape during footy matches and why they always have to have the loudest burp.

⭐ They talk differently when they're with their mates – it's a code made up of grunts that binds them together. Uh? Yuh. Sorted!

⭐ They brag and exaggerate (and lie) to their mates about everything in order to be seen as the coolest/sexiest/toughest.

She was **gagging** for it!!!

GET THIS!
On average, girls learn to talk earlier than boys.

Q My friends say I'm pretty, but boys don't seem to fancy me. What am I doing wrong?

Nothing, probably – maybe they're the wrong kind of boys! But just in case, check you're not guilty of committing a typical girly-crime that turns boys off.

12 THINGS GIRLS DO THAT BOYS HATE:

1. Go to the toilet together
2. Wear weird clothes and too much make-up
3. Laugh like donkeys to get attention
4. Spend hours getting ready
5. Cry in public
6. Act dumb
7. Agree with everything he says
8. Treat him like a kid
9. Discuss his secrets with their mates
10. Stalk him
11. Show him up in public
12. Keep asking, "Do you love me?"

GET THIS!
In conversations, most girls want to know "Why?" while most boys want to know "How?"

Q How can you tell if a boy fancies you or not?

The last thing he's going to do is tell you, in case you laugh, tell your mates or suggest he takes a running jump. If he teases you, gives you a nickname or kicks your chair away, he probably fancies you rotten; but mostly he'll tell you via his body language. Here are some dead giveaways...

BOY BODY LANGUAGE FOR
"I FANCY YOU"

* Furtive glances

* Sneaky smiles

* Acting cool

* Showing off

Look at **ME!**

* Copying the way you sit

* Touching his hair

* Eye contact

* Being horrible

HOW TO SAY
"I FANCY YOU"
BACK

* Flutter your eyelashes (but don't overdo it or you'll just look mental).

* Hold his gaze for a few secs, then look away.

* Smile back mysteriously.

* Tell your mate to tell his mate to tell him.

* Lend him your best pen in Geography.

* Give him your last chip.

* Stand on a chair with a rose between your teeth (ha ha!).

* Flick your hair.

Q Help! I'm really shy with boys - I don't know how to talk to them.

The main thing is to be yourself - if you're not sure who that is yet, here are some ways of behaving that boys like:

♥ Listen to him and look interested.

♥ Ask his advice.

♥ Be happy - he won't want to hang out with a whinger.

♥ Make him laugh.

♥ Stand up straight, walk with confidence (you're a princess!).

♥ Praise him! Cheer if he scores or tell him he was robbed if he loses.

♥ Find out what he's into and talk to him about it.

♥ Be mysterious - he doesn't want to know about the boil on your bum.

Q I fancy a boy I play tennis with. I know he likes me, but he won't make the first move – is it OK for me to ask him out?

If he won't play ball but fancies the frilly pants off you, go for it. Here's some tips:

1. Pick your moment. Don't ask him to "play doubles" in front of his mates or he might just smack you round the head with his racket – no score.

2. Keep it casual – as in "Fancy going to the pictures/bungee jumping/up the chippy later?" (The ball is now in his court.)

3. If he says "no", stay cool and say that a load of you were going anyway. Don't beg or cry – there'll be other ace players.

4. If he says "yes", don't wrap your arms and legs round him and give him a big, wet kiss – look like it happens every day and ask when he's free. Game, set and match!

First date tips

He's asked you out, he's lush, and the last thing you want to do is blow it. But is that spinach on your teeth? Check out this list...

BEFORE YOU GO

☐ ARE YOU WEARING SCARY CLOTHES? (Boys don't mind other girls looking crazy or tarty – but not their dates.)

☐ HAVE YOU REMEMBERED TO WEAR DEODORANT?

☐ IS YOUR BREATH FRESH? (Carry mints/breath fresheners with you.)

☐ HAVE YOU GOT SCUM/LIPSTICK/FOOD ON YOUR TEETH?

☐ IS YOUR MAKE-UP OTT? (Do you look like a drag queen?)

☐ HAVE YOU GOT A BOGEY UP YOUR NOSE?

☐ IS YOUR SKIRT CAUGHT IN YOUR KNICKERS? (Look at your rear view in the mirror.)

☐ ARE YOU WEARING YOUR BEST UNDERWEAR? (Grey bra straps are grim.)

☐ ARE YOU WEARING TOO MUCH PERFUME? (A light mist only – it's not flyspray.)

ON THE DATE...

If you don't fancy him, at least be kind – say thank you and a quick bye.

Turn up on time and remember his name – don't call him Kevin if it's Colin.

Meet somewhere neutral so your dad can't give him the Spanish Inquisition.

If you bump into his mates, be friendly and smile sweetly but don't get clingy.

Tell him he looks nice – he'll have made an effort, even if it doesn't show.

If there's a ghastly silence, ask him about something he's into and make it so he can't just answer yes or no. Hopefully it'll get a conversation going.

If he hugs you and you want him to kiss you, look him in the eye – boys usually read that as encouragement.

Offer to pay your way, but if he insists on paying, let him.

KNOW A GOOD DATE FROM A BAD ONE

🙂 He missed the cup final for you.

🙂🙂 He's had a tattoo of your name.

🙂🙂 He sucked off your indelible lipstick.

🙂🙂🙂 He gave you his grandma's engagement ring.

🙂🙂 He cried when you left.

🙁 You fell asleep while he was talking.

🙁🙁 He brought his mum with him.

🙁🙁 He said he fancied your best mate.

🙁🙁🙁 His girlfriend turned up and hit you with her handbag.

🙁🙁🙁 He made you feel small, ugly and stupid.

HOW TO DUMP HIM

You're **DUMPED**, sucker!

"Breaking up is hard to do", according to ancient but very accurate lyrics. If you know you've come to the end of the line with a guy, it's not easy to tell him, especially if he's done nothing wrong and thinks everything is rosy. If he's been a complete creep and has done something hideous, you're allowed to tell him to get stuffed through a megaphone in the high street. But if you've just stopped loving him, do it gently. There are several ways...

✓ Go to a neutral location and tell him straight: you don't think this is working out; you need space; it's not him, it's you ... anything to cushion the blow.

✓ If you really can't face him, grab your pen and write him a letter.

✓ If he lives a long way away, a phone call is OK-ish, but if he's very upset you may not get a chance to finish what you meant to say.

✗ Don't text or e-mail the big heave-ho. If he's been bad, fine. If not, it can come across as cold and uncaring. Don't add insult to injury.

✗ Don't get one of your gozzy mates to tell him – how humiliating is that?!

✓ If he won't take no for an answer, change your mobile number, be "out" when he calls round and let it slip that you have a new (very large) boyfriend.

Worst Case Scenario

HELP! My boyfriend's dumped me. I love him soooo much. How can I ever get over him?

OUCH, it hurts! You thought you meant everything to him and you still don't know where you went wrong. Was it something you did or said? The way you look? Being dumped can leave you feeling like the most unlovable person on the planet. But hang on! This is one guy's opinion. You might look like crap now because you've been crying, but you've had a relationship with someone. He fancied you! Which means you *are* lovable and attractive. Being dumped doesn't have to mean there's something wrong with you – it's the relationship that was wrong. What you need now is a plan of action...

Action plan

1. GET HIM OUT OF YOUR SYSTEM

❤ Close the curtains, play "your song", lie on the bed and cry and cry. Do not look in the mirror.

❤ Run a bath and relax with chocolate.

❤ Go to bed. Tomorrow is the first day of the rest of your life.

2. GET ANGRY WITH HIM

❤ Stamp on his photo. Tear up his letters and throw them in the bin.

❤ Write a list of all his faults – nobody's perfect. See him for what he was!

3. GET OVER HIM

❤ Spoil yourself! Get your hair done, buy a new top and some new make-up.

❤ Ring your best mate and make plans.

❤ Go out, have fun – and forget him!

NB It can take time to mend a broken heart, depending on your situation. If the sadness is going on for too long and you can't cope, see your doctor – she knows how to help.

Q Help! My date said he'd call but that was over a week ago!

If he likes you, he'll call, but give him at least a fortnight – he won't want to lose his cool by seeming too keen. If he doesn't ring, he may have taken your number out of politeness – it's kinder than telling a girl she's not his type. No matter how desperate you feel, don't sit by the phone. Go out, have fun! If you're not in when he calls, he'll think you're dead popular and he'll hunt you down!

Q I went to see a boy band and the lead singer winked at me. I love him so much, I can't stop crying.

Too much hanky and no panky can be truly upsetting. Having a crush on a celeb is so normal, even your nan had one. It's good for working out which kind of guy you fancy, but the chances of you walking down the aisle with him are pretty slim, painful as that seems. Is he really the boy for you? You haven't a clue what he's like as a person. Dance to his music but don't waste your tears on him!

Q I don't want a boyfriend yet – am I abnormal?

No! Nobody "needs" a boyfriend and happiness does not depend on having one. The whole point of hanging out with boys is for fun, but if you've got lots of other fun things to do right now, keep doing 'em! If and when you decide to have a relationship, you'll be a much more interesting person for it. Besides, being single means you're always free to see your mates, no one can be unfaithful to you and you can flirt with whoever you like!

Q What's a lesbian?

It's a girl who finds girls sexually attractive instead of boys. However, many girls with boyfriends fantasize about sex with other girls – it's human nature to be curious. Understanding your own sexuality can be confusing, especially when you're young. While some people know for sure that they're "gay" or "straight", loads of us hover in-between.

LESBIAN (HOMOSEXUAL, GAY, DYKE): A girl who only fancies girls.

BI-CURIOUS: Someone who'd like to get physical with someone of the same sex to see what it's like.

BISEXUAL: Someone who fancies people of both sexes.

HETEROSEXUAL: Someone who fancies people of the opposite sex.

Q Why are some people gay?

Nobody knows for sure. Some think it's genetic – you are either born gay or you're not. Some think it's to do with upbringing and that something in your life makes you "decide" to be gay. Others reckon it's a combination of factors – there's no real proof either way. We're all attracted to different people, and who we fancy may be more to do with our partner's personality than whether they are male or female.

Q What's homophobia?

It means being frightened of, or not liking, homosexuals. Some people think being gay is "unnatural" or "a sin against God". There are even a few intolerant sickos who beat gay people up (queer-bashing). So should you admit you're gay, or not? Some think you should come "out" and be proud. Others think that what you do in private is nobody else's business. In the end, it's down to the individual. Sadly, some gay people feel so ashamed, they commit suicide. This is never, ever the answer. They deserve the same love and respect as straight people. If you're gay and having a tough time, there are plenty of like-minded people who understand and can help. Call them. (See page 80 for a helpline.)

Q Help! I've got a boyfriend but I don't know how to kiss him!

The usual advice is to "do what comes naturally" – bad advice if that means clamping your lips onto his nose or using your tongue like a windscreen-wiper. If your boy hasn't passed his kissing exams either, he may lunge and suck your contact lens out by accident or clamp you by the bottom lip until it goes blue. Don't despair – there is an art to kissing. Pucker up and practise!

How to kiss for beginners

OK, here we go. Put one arm round his waist and the other on his shoulder, or both round his shoulders (not his throat!).

1. Hold him close, then make eye contact.

2. Place your slightly opened mouth lightly against his. (No sudden movements.)

3. Move your mouth slightly in time with his. (Slowly – you're not a goldfish!)

4. Remember to breathe through your nose – bulgy eyes isn't a good look. Close them if you want.

5. Gently suck his lips with yours if you like – but don't make like you're vacuuming the hall.

6. If you use your tongue, be subtle – give him a kiss, not a tonsillectomy.

7. If you dribble, burp or gag, make a joke of it.

Q *Help! I missed the sex video at school, so I'm a bit behind on boys' dangly bits.*

Boys all have the same basic equipment, but like girls, they come in many shapes and sizes. The biggest difference between boys and us is that they wear their major baby-making equipment on the outside – show-offs!

BOYS' BITS

1. TESTICLES (balls, nuts, knackers, bollocks): These make male sex cells, called sperm.

2. SCROTUM (ball bag, nad sack): Loose pouch of wrinkled skin which hangs outside body and contains testicles.

3. EPIDIDYMIS: Coiled tube where sperm mature. Links testicle to sperm duct.

4. SPERM DUCTS: Carry sperm towards the penis.

5. SEMINAL VESICLES: Glands producing fluid that gives sperm energy.

6. PROSTATE GLAND: Produces fluid which helps sperm move.

7. URETHRA: Carries urine and sperm (but not at the same time).

8. PENIS (willy, knob, cock, dick, prick): Small and soft until sexually excited, then it grows, becomes stiff (erect) and stands away from the body, allowing it to fit into a vagina during sex.

9. GLANS (bell end, helmet): Tip of the penis – the most sensitive part.

10. FORESKIN: Fold of skin that covers glans. Glands underneath produce white creamy stuff called smegma. This helps the skin slide smoothly over the glans. It can get very smelly if not washed regularly. Sometimes the foreskin is removed for religious or medical reasons (called circumcision).

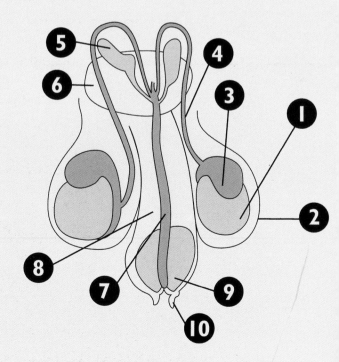

The Great Big Willy page

Q How big is the average willy?

Rulers ready? When the average penis is soft and floppy (flaccid) it measures about 6–10 cm long. When it's erect, it's 12–17 cm long and 3–4 cm thick.

Q What's an erection?

A stiff penis (or "hard-on", in boy-speak). Willies are made of body tissue full of blood vessels. When a boy is turned on, blood pumps into the vessels and his penis goes hard and stands up. Erections can happen at any time – they're not always caused by sexy thoughts. This can be deeply embarrassing if it's unwanted, so do the ladylike thing and pretend not to notice – the boy can't help it.

Q What's ejaculation?

When semen (spunk) squirts out of an erect penis. Semen contains a cocktail of sperm and fluid and there's usually about a teaspoonful each time. It can be any shade from greyish to white to yellow, and when it comes out, it's warm. Ejaculation happens during an orgasm (when he comes/has a climax), usually when the penis is stimulated through sex or masturbation (see page 110). During orgasm, muscles round the bladder tighten so that no urine can come out with the semen.

Q My virgin boyfriend's got a spot on his willy – why?

Genitals get spots and rashes just like faces and they usually go away on their own. Warts are different – they can be caught by having sex with someone who's got them, but virgin boys can get them too. They should see a doctor for treatment.
NB Un-treated genital warts can be passed on to girls through sex and may cause cervical cancer later on.

Wart do you think it is???

107

What's its name?

Boys love their dick as much as their dog – they stroke it, pet it and, yes, they even give it a name. Here are some of the most common ones:

~~Weiner~~

Knob

Dick

Willy

Chopper

John Thomas

Winkle

Percy

Whanger

Sausage

Prick

Tool

Todger

Cock

Shlong

Truncheon

Dong

AND NOW: A LOAD OF BALLS

From puberty, sperm forms continuously in the testicles – which is why guys old enough to be your grandpa can still become daddies! They are the most sensitive part of the male body – to be knocked in the knackers is the most excruciating of pains (we'll never know, will we ladies?). Boys often worry that one testicle is bigger or hangs lower than the other, but hardly anyone has a truly matching pair.

Q What is a wet dream?

This is when boys ejaculate in their sleep. If it's going to happen (and it doesn't always) it's usually around the age of 12–15. It can come as a shock if they don't know what's going on, and lots of boys think they've wet themselves or that there's something wrong with their dick. But it's just nature's way of getting rid of excess sperm.

Q Is semen poisonous?

No – you could have it on toast if you wanted, but be aware that you can get STDs (sexually transmitted diseases) from semen if your partner is infected.

Hold onto your knicker elastic, girls ...
here comes

THE SEXY SECTION

Q Help! When I see a boy I fancy, I feel all tingly inside.

When your sex hormones start working, you become aware of new sensations in your mind and body. Here are some feelings you might experience:

✪ Boys who you used to find gross suddenly seem ... cute!

✪ Your knees turn to jelly when a certain boy walks past.

✪ You find yourself staring at boys when you go swimming.

✪ You suddenly feel shy with a boy you've played with since nursery.

✪ You get a crush on someone in a band and want to have all his babies.

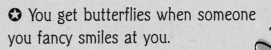

✪ You dream about snogging your hunky PE teacher.

✪ You get butterflies when someone you fancy smiles at you.

✪ You have a desperate urge to be kissed and touched – all over!

✪ You can't stop thinking about someone you fancy.

✪ You don't know whether you want to cry or laugh.

Q Help! Sometimes I have really sexy dreams about boys I don't know.

Great, isn't it? Everyone has them, don't worry! Lie back and enjoy. The good thing about sexy dreams and fantasies is that you can do whatever you like with whoever you want and nobody gets hurt.

Q What's masturbation?

Masturbation (wanking, tossing off) is when you touch your genitals for pleasure and sexual relief. Most people do it, each in their own sweet way, often until they have an orgasm (see page 107). Even animals do it. Masturbation doesn't make you go blind or harm you in any way. In fact, it's a good way of getting to know yourself. It's only a problem if you become obsessed and don't do anything else! (But the same could be said for stamp-collecting.)

How girls do it:

Some girls rub their clitoris and/or insert a penis-like object into their vagina (finger, vibrator, etc.). Others use water from a shower-head to tickle their fancy – the possibilities are endless.

OOOH, MMM, I'm just having a shower!

There are two golden rules:

a) Only do it in private.
b) Never use dangerous objects as sex toys – e.g. glass bottles or anything sharp, dirty or likely to break or get stuck inside you.

How boys do it:

For many boys, masturbation is a major hobby. They touch their privates every time they pee, so it's a small leap to give themselves a hand-job. How? Most boys hold their penis and rub it rhythmically until they ejaculate. Like girls, some feel guilty about it, but there's no need.

Q What's an orgasm (coming, having a climax)?

It's a series of little muscular spasms that gives you a feeling of fantastic sexual pleasure. It normally happens when your genitals are stimulated during masturbation or sex. When it happens, your heart beats faster, the sensation spreads through your body and you may feel as if you're floating. Orgasms build to a peak then ebb away after a few seconds, leaving you relaxed and possibly sleepy. In boys, orgasm ends in ejaculation.

Q When my boyfriend nibbles my ear, it really turns me on – how come?

Ears are erogenous zones! An erogenous zone is any part of the body that's sexually sensitive to touch – which includes being nibbled, kissed, stroked, licked, squeezed or tickled with a feather, if that's what turns you on. Different girls have different places where they like to be touched.

Q What's heavy petting (foreplay, touching up)?

It's sexual kissing and touching and can include kissing with tongues, him touching your breasts, touching each other's genitals or "dry humping" (boy-speak for rubbing against each other as if you're having sex, only with all your clothes on). This kind of touching creates feelings of intense pleasure and a desire to have sex.

WARNING!
When you're all loved-up like this, it's very hard to stop. If you're not ready to have sex or don't want to for whatever reason, make it clear to your partner from the beginning. If you forget, get carried away or change your mind, you can still say no to sex at any stage.

Crap things boys say to get you into bed

But I really love you.
(So why's he putting pressure on you like that?)

It'll prove how much you love me.
(He'd say the same if he wanted one of your crisps.)

I can't wait for ever.
(Oh, please! He's known you 5 minutes!)

It'll prove you're not frigid.
(What – is he a doctor or something?)

I'll dump you if you don't.
(He's dumped already, right?)

But my balls will turn blue!
(Good – they'll match his video collection.)

111

Q What's sexual intercourse?

Sexual intercourse is when a man puts his penis inside a woman's vagina and slides it in and out until he ejaculates. It can take over an hour or a few seconds.

Q Does losing your virginity hurt?

Some girls feel little or no pain, but it can be a bit sore if you have a tight or unbroken hymen (the thin layer of skin covering the vaginal opening). You may also bleed slightly. Also, if you are tense or nervous, your vagina will be tighter and dryer. Try using a lubricant like KY Jelly (from the chemist – often near the condom display) and take things slowly. The next time will be less painful.

Q What's oral sex?

Licking, sucking or kissing someone's genitals. When it's done to a guy, the proper word is fellatio (feh-lay-shee-oh). Slang expressions are Giving Head, Going Down On or giving a Blow Job. When it's done to a girl, it's called cunnilingus (cunny-ling-gus). Slang expressions are Licking Out, Eating and Going Down On.

Q What's anal sex?

Putting an erect penis, finger or other object up your bum hole (anus). The tissues inside the rectum can be easily damaged, so any activity in this area should be very gentle. Anal sex is highly risky because it may cause bleeding, and blood can carry diseases. Use a condom and never put anything that's been up your bum into your mouth or vagina.

GET THIS!
Many of us are virgins when we get married.

Other names for sexual intercourse (rudest last)

What Granny calls it:

doing it   having it away

how's your father

you-know-what

making whoopee   a bit of the other

What your mum calls it:

making love   having sex

sleeping with

going to bed with   intercourse

What the vicar calls it:

copulating   mating

conjugal rights

fornicating

consummating marriage vows

What boys call it:

fucking

shagging   screwing

knobbing   giving her one

getting laid   poking

THE 3 Ps – 3 things every girl should know before she has sex

POLICE: In Britain, it is illegal to have sex if you're under 16. The law is there to protect under-age kids from abuse, and anyone caught having sex with someone under 16 could be charged.

PREGNANT: If you don't use contraception, you could get pregnant. Make sure you know how to use it and what to do if it fails (see pages 117–120).

POX: You could catch an STD (sexually transmitted disease). It's not very romantic, but there are some serious diseases that can be caught by having sex with someone who is infected. Some STDs don't produce symptoms for months, which means you could have a disease, not know you've got it and pass it on to someone else. The best way to protect yourself and your partner is to use a condom every time you have sex.

Sexually transmitted diseases

If you think you may have an infection, see your doctor for advice.

What	How	Symptoms	Cure
CHLAMYDIA	Vaginal sex/touching genitals then touching your eyes	Most women won't notice any but may have vaginal discharge, frequent or painful weeing, stomache ache, pain during sex, irregular bleeding, sore eyes.	Antibiotics (if not treated, can lead to infertility)
GENITAL HERPES Type 1: sores on the nose/mouth Type 2: sores on genitals/anus	Kissing; oral, vaginal or anal sex	Itching, tingling around mouth/genitals. Blisters develop which burst and leave painful sores. Possible flu-like symptoms. During this time, all sexual contact should be avoided.	NONE – attacks can re-occur at any time
GENITAL WARTS Small fleshy growths that grow near genitals/anus	Contact with genitals; vaginal, anal or oral sex	Some can be almost invisible, others resemble tiny cauliflowers. May itch. Can cause cancer in women, so best treated on discovery.	Podophyllin (a paint-on solution), freezing or laser treatment
GONORRHOEA (CLAP)	Vaginal, anal or oral sex	Not always. Sometimes painful weeing/sore throat. A rash can develop which affects the nervous system.	Penicillin
HIV AND AIDS HIV = Human Immunodeficiency Virus, which attacks the immune system. An infected person is known as HIV positive but may stay well for years before they develop AIDS. AIDS = Acquired Immune Deficiency Syndrome, which is a collection of illnesses/ conditions that occur when the body is weakened by HIV.	Vaginal, anal or oral sex	HIV: night sweats, fever, lack of energy, diarrhoea, weight loss, thrush, herpes, dry skin and rashes, mouth ulcers and beeding gums. AIDS: breathing problems, eyesight problems, brain problems, cancer.	NONE – although therapies and medical research are advancing all the time
HEPATITIS B Viral infection of the liver – more infectious than HIV	Sexual contact; through blood or saliva with blood in	Lack of energy and appetite, fever, jaundiced skin, yellowing of whites of eyes, pale poo, dark wee, abdominal pain.	NONE – but some recover after rest

Q Help! I'm in love but I'm not sure whether to have sex with my boyfriend.

You love him – he loves you. You've gone past first base, had a steamy snog and no doubt a case of the wandering hands. It's time to ask yourself some serious questions:

1. DO YOU HONESTLY BELIEVE YOU ARE BOTH IN LOVE?

If he's not in love with you, he could break your heart like a cracker biscuit. If you're only doing it because all your mates have, don't! You only lose your virginity once – shame if you can't remember where you put it!

2. CAN YOU TALK TO HIM ABOUT SEX?

If you end up giggling and avoiding the issue, you're not ready – that's fine. If you're not confident enough to tell him to stop, avoid being alone with him for now. Give it time.

3. DO YOU TRUST HIM?

You need to be able to trust him 100%. Sex makes us vulnerable, physically and emotionally. It's normal to feel nervous the first time, but if your partner frightens you, suggests things you don't want to do or doesn't respect you, say no before you get hurt.

4. HAVE YOU DISCUSSED CONTRACEPTION?

You really have to talk about this – he may assume you've sorted it and are on the pill. You may think he'll bring condoms, but what if he doesn't? If neither of you is mature enough to sort out decent contraception, who's going to be responsible for the baby?

5. HOW LONG HAVE YOU KNOWN HIM?

Love (and lust) can happen at first sight, but it's best to get to know the guy for a while before you jump into bed.

6. DO YOU KNOW HOW TO HAVE SAFE SEX?

Using condoms is the best protection against STDs. If you don't know your boyfriend's sexual history and he refuses to wear a condom, refuse to have sex with him – it sounds mean, but giving someone a poxy disease is worse.

IF YOU DO DECIDE TO HAVE SEX, plan ahead to make it safe and special. Find somewhere private, take your time and don't expect too much first go. It takes two to tango (and you'll know when you've been tango-ed).

Shall we?

Shan't we?

PREGNANCY

To get pregnant, all you need to do is have sex without using contraception. If your boyfriend is fertile (chances are, he is) and you're fertile (and you could be ovulating even before your first period) it's possible to get pregnant the very first time you have sex – you can never be too careful. Around 90,000 teenage girls get caught out every year in Britain.

HOW PREGNANCY (conception) HAPPENS

When a man ejaculates inside a woman's vagina, hundreds of millions of sperm cells are deposited near the cervix.

Sperm swim through the uterus into the uterine tubes.

If there's an ovum (egg) in one of the tubes, sperm cluster around it and one may join it. This is conception. Together, ovum and sperm make one new cell, which develops into a baby.

Don't believe the myths!

You can get pregnant if the man withdraws before he comes...

You can get pregnant the first time you have sex...

You can get pregnant if you have sex standing up...

You can get pregnant if you have sex during your period...

You can get pregnant if you pee straight after sex...

You can get pregnant if you don't have an orgasm...

IMPOSSIBLE! We were standing up!

How not to get pregnant

Lots of girls want to be mums one day but most would rather start a family when they're good and ready. You have a choice: if you don't want to get pregnant, you can either say no to sex for now, or decide to use contraception.

What	How	Where	Pros	Cons
CONDOM (johnny, rubber) A thin latex covering that fits over the erect penis (disposable)	It catches sperm and stops it entering the vagina. 86% effective if used properly.	Cheaply from shops. Free from family-planning clinics and doctors.	The best prevention against STDs except for saying no	Can split/tear. You have to interrupt sex to put it on.
DIAPHRAGM/CERVICAL CAP A washable latex dome that fits inside the vagina and covers the cervix. Check for holes!	Used with spermicide it kills sperm/prevents them entering cervix. 80–90% effective.	They have to be fitted at the family-planning clinic/doctor's.	Doesn't interrupt sex as you can put it in 1–2 hours before	Can be fiddly to put in. Must stay in place 6–8 hours after sex.
SPERMICIDE A cream, gel, foam or pessary inserted into the vagina/used with other methods to make them more effective	Contains chemicals that kills sperm. 72–94% effective.	Chemist, doctor's	Reduces the risk of pregnancy when used with other methods	Not reliable used alone. Can be messy. Can cause skin allergy.
BIRTH CONTROL PILL A pill that controls hormones. (Two main types with different dosages.) Not advised for smokers.	One contains progesterone, which prevents ovulation. The other contains progestin, which makes the uterus unsuitable for an egg. 95–99% effective.	On prescription	Very effective against pregnancy. Possibly lighter, less painful periods.	You must take it regularly. Can cause side-effects: nausea, headache, bloating, weight gain, breast tenderness and depression.
IUD A plastic/copper device that fits inside the uterus	Prevents egg from settling in uterus. 98–99% effective.	They have to be fitted at the family-planning clinic/doctor's.	Can be kept in place for years. Can't feel it.	Can cause infection. Not recommended if you haven't had children.

EARLY SIGNS OF PREGNANCY

These start about 2 weeks after conception and can include a missed period, morning sickness and tender breasts.

Missing a period might not mean you're pregnant, but if you've had sex without using contraception and you're late, do a pregnancy test. Kits can be bought at the chemist. They're easy to use and accurate if you use them properly. If you are pregnant, don't kid yourself it isn't happening.

Worst Case Scenario
HELP! I think I may be pregnant.
I don't know what to do.

If you forget to take the pill or a condom splits, you can get "morning after" pills from the doctor, family-planning clinic or over the counter at the chemist. As long as you take them within 72 hours of having sex, they usually stop you getting pregnant. These are for emergency use only – never use them as a method of contraception.

If you've left it too late and a pregnancy test indicates that you really are pregnant, don't despair. You're not the first girl it's happened to and you won't be the last. You're not dirty, evil or a slag. Accidents happen to women much older and wiser than you. Don't be scared of telling your mum – most mums will do everything they can to help their pregnant daughters. If she blows a fuse, you can bet it's because she blames herself in some way. (Nuts, but there it is.) She'll also be worried for you. If you really can't face your parents yet, you still need to tell someone fast because apart from a cuddle, you'll need help and advice to decide what to do next.

People you could talk to:

Mum or Dad; one of Mum's friends that you trust; a close relative (a favourite auntie, maybe); a teacher you really like; your doctor; the school nurse; your boyfriend. There are lots of people who will help you and not judge you.

What are your options?

✪ You can keep the baby.
✪ You can have it adopted.
✪ You can have an abortion.

Whatever you decide, each option has consequences that will affect your life in the future. Don't try and go it alone.

BEING A TEEN MUM

Bringing up a baby is really hard work. It's even harder if you're in your teens, you're single and the pregnancy wasn't planned. Some girls cope brilliantly (it's not all doom and gloom!) but others have a tough time – here are some of the reasons they give:

✳ You lose your freedom – babies need care 24/7, leaving you little time to go out.

✳ Boredom, loneliness and depression.

✳ You may have to survive on benefits – and babies and childcare are expensive.

✳ Your studies may have to go on hold.

✳ Where will you live? Most teenage mums don't end up living with the baby's father.

✳ Single mums have trouble finding boyfriends – it's harder to meet Mr Right.

WHAT'S AN ABORTION?

ABORTION IS AN OPERATION to end a pregnancy. It's sometimes also called a termination. It involves removing the developing foetus from the womb by suction, scraping or with medication, depending on how advanced the pregnancy is. An abortion must always be performed by a registered doctor in a clinic or hospital – abortion clinics can be found in the telephone directory but it's best to be referred by your GP. Before an abortion is allowed two doctors must agree that having a baby would harm the mother's physical or mental health, or that it would be disabled.

In Britain, abortion is legal up to the 24th week of pregnancy but it's safest to have the operation in the early stages of pregnancy (within the first 3 months). Many doctors are unwilling to perform late abortions, for moral and medical reasons.

Having an abortion can screw you up emotionally – while some girls just feel relieved that it's over, others have regrets and need support. If you're not sure whether to go ahead or not, ask to speak to a counsellor and find out as much as you can about the procedure.

SEXUAL ABUSE

Sex with someone you love can be fantastic – but sex is only good if you want it to happen. Few girls get through life without some boy trying it on – it can be upsetting, but it's often to do with the boy being immature. A sharp remark and a firm "NO!" should stop him.

The much nastier threat comes from pervy adults who use their power to make you do intimate stuff you don't want to do. The person could be a stranger or someone you know, like a neighbour or a relative. Whoever they are, there's *no way* they should be doing it. It's illegal for anyone to force you to have sex, touch you against your will or make unwanted sexual remarks. If you're under 16 it's even more serious.

If it happens, tell an adult you trust to make sure it stops. If your mum can't deal with it, tell your teacher. Don't be frightened to tell, even if you've promised not to. You've done nothing wrong – *they* have! Get help fast.

SAFETY TIPS FOR STREETWISE CHICKS

✪ Walk with friends whenever you can – there's safety in numbers.

✪ If you're walking any distance on your own, wear shoes you can run in.

✪ Avoid alleys, underpasses, stairwells and multi-storey car parks at night and stay in well-lit, busy areas. Don't take short-cuts through woods, fields or parks.

✪ Know where you're going – if you act lost, you're an easy target.

✪ Never hitch lifts – even in company.

✪ Stay away from the kerb. If a stranger kerb-crawls you, don't talk to him.

✪ Don't wear headphones – you won't hear anyone coming up behind you.

✪ Never give out your real name, address, phone number or school to anyone over the Internet, even if they seem genuine.

✪ If you're followed or approached, go to the nearest house/shop or stop a female passer-by. Tell them what's wrong and ask them to call the police or your parents. Incidentally, if you just scream for help people tend to ignore you – calling "fire" or "rape" is more likely to get attention.

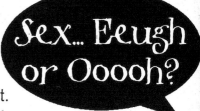

Sex... Eeugh or Ooooh?

IT SOMETIMES seems like everyone is having sex or talking about it. When you're young, the subject may seem so gross that you never want to go there. But sex isn't all about diseases and unwanted babies. Good, loving sex never feels smutty, slutty or scary. Sex with a partner who loves and respects you is fantastic! It makes you feel wanted. It makes you feel good. And hey, it's fun! Yes, be careful. Yes, know the facts. Then, when you feel ready and old enough and you're truly, madly, deeply in love, lie back and enjoy it! Or swing off the chandelier together. Whatever turns you on.

Where next?
For further advice, check out these websites:

Bullying
ChildLine: www.childline.org.uk
Bully UK: www.bullying.co.uk

Drugs
National Drugs Helpline: www.talktofrank.com

Growing Up
Being Girl: www.beinggirl.co.uk
Tampax: www.tampax.co.uk

Make Up
Lauren Luke tutorials: www.bylaurenluke.com

Personal Safety
Live Life Safe: www.livelifesafe.org.uk

Sexual Health
FPA: www.fpa.org.uk
Marie Stopes: www.mariestopes.org.uk

Sexuality
London Lesbian & Gay Switchboard: www.llgs.org.uk
Lesbian Gay Bisexual Transgender Youth Scotland:
www.lgbtyouth.org.uk

Keep a record here of other useful websites, phone numbers, tips and tricks your friends have shared:

INDEX

Check out these books for more brilliant information:

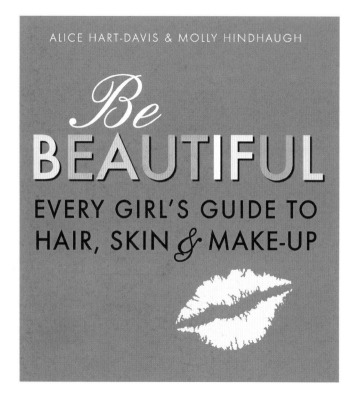

Be Beautiful
978-1-4063-1831-9

A practical and comprehensive beauty guide for teen girls by an award-winning beauty journalist.

Know Your Brain
978-1-4063-0415-2

Find out everything there is to know about your brain in this fascinating grey-matter guide!

Blame My Brain

978-1-4063-1116-7

A comprehensive guide to the biological
mysteries that lie behind teenage behaviour.

Leaving Home Survival Guide

978-1-4063-8442-8771-0

This indispensible reference book contains everything
a young adult will need to know when leaving the nest.

Bits, Boobs & Blobs,
Zits, Glitz & Body Blitz,
Snogs, Sex & Soulmates first published 2004
by Walker Books Ltd, 87 Vauxhall Walk, London SE11 5HJ
This compendium edition published 2010

2 4 6 8 10 9 7 5 3 1

This book has been typeset in Clichee, Alghera and Tree Boxelder
Printed in Singapore

British Library Cataloguing in Publication Data:
a catalogue record for this book is available from the British Library

ISBN 978-1-4063-2367-2

WALKER BOOKS
AND SUBSIDIARIES
LONDON · BOSTON · SYDNEY · AUCKLAND

www.walker.co.uk